# 1989: END OF THE TWENTIETH CENTURY

## A NORTON DOCUMENTS READER

**NORTON DOCUMENTS READER SERIES**

*The Age of Jim Crow*
by Jane Dailey

*The Global Revolutions of 1968*
by Jeremi Suri

*Indian Removal*
by David S. Heidler and Jeanne T. Heidler

*Two Communities in the Civil War*
by Andrew J. Torget and Edward L. Ayers

*Pirates in the Age of Sail*
by Robert Antony

**FORTHCOMING TITLES INCLUDE**

*Reforming America, 1815–1860*
by Joshua D. Rothman

*The Mongols and Global History*
by Morris Rossabi

# 1989: END OF THE TWENTIETH CENTURY

---

A NORTON DOCUMENTS READER

---

*James Carter*
*Cynthia Paces*

W. W. NORTON & COMPANY

*New York / London*

Manufacturing by the Courier Companies—Westford division
Series design by Jo Anne Metsch
Production manager: Eric Pier-Hocking

Library of Congress Cataloging-in-Publication Data

Carter, James Hugh.
    1989 : end of the twentieth century : a Norton documents reader / James Carter, Cynthia Paces. — 1st ed.
       p. cm. — (Norton documents reader series)
    Includes bibliographical references and index.

    ISBN 978-0-393-93066-5 (pbk.)

    1. Nineteen eighty-nine, A.D. 2. History, Modern—1989- 3. World politics—1985-1995. 4. Revolutions—History—20th century. 5. Social change—History—20th century. 6. International relations—History—20th century. I. Paces, Cynthia. II. Title.
    D856.C376 2009

    909.82'8—dc22

                          2009023919

W. W. Norton & Company, Inc., 500 Fifth Avenue, New York, N.Y. 10110
www.wwnorton.com

W. W. Norton & Company Ltd., Castle House, 75/76 Wells Street, London W1T 3QT
1 2 3 4 5 6 7 8 9 0

# CONTENTS

# ACKNOWLEDGMENTS

The events of 1989 have of course been fundamental to the recent histories of China and East Central Europe. As scholars of China and East-Central Europe, respectively, both authors have benefited from countless discussions with colleagues and friends about these events. Specific to the writing and compiling of this book, James would like to thank Sue McFadden and Chris Klosko for help compiling and arranging the documents, and his spring 2008 seminar students at Saint Joseph's University. Cynthia would like to thank Jo-Ann Gross, Matt Bender, and the Support of Scholarly Activities (SOSA) program at The College of New Jersey.

# Part I

# Introduction

## One Revolution of the Earth

> In Poland it took ten years, in Hungary ten months, in East Germany ten weeks: perhaps in Czechoslovakia it will take ten days![1]

A videotape of an elfin-looking academic, hoisting a beer in a Prague pub as he predicted the rapid demise of communism, circulated on news broadcasts throughout the world in November 1989. In a scene unthinkable just a few months earlier, the British historian and journalist Timothy Garton Ash shared drinks with dissident leaders while thousands of Czechoslovaks occupied the frigid squares of their capital city, for decades the seat of one of the world's most repressive communist regimes. But in 1989 the unexpected appeared regularly on the world's TV screens. CNN, the first twenty-four-hour cable news network, was less than a decade old and was broadcasting images of stunning change: jubilant Berliners tearing down the Wall dividing their city; a lone Chinese man halting a column of tanks near Tiananmen Square; South African dissidents walking free after two decades in prison; elections in Poland, Panama, Chile, and Argentina; Romanian dictator Nicolae Ceaușescu and his wife Elena executed on Christmas Day, lying in pools of their own blood.

The "Velvet Revolution" in Czechoslovakia took a bit longer than the ten days Garton Ash predicted, but the tide came in fast. No one seemed prepared for how quickly communist governments,

---

[1] Timothy Garton Ash, *The Magic Lantern: The Revolution of '89 Witnessed in Warsaw, Budapest, Berlin, and Prague* (New York: Vintage Books, reprint edition, 1993), 78.

1

entrenched since just after World War II, peacefully gave up power. Even scholars, normally wary of romanticizing events, saw the end of communist hegemony in Eastern Europe as magical. Colorful photographs of punk-fashioned students with chisels at the Berlin Wall added to the fantastic atmosphere of late 1989. Padraic Kenney called 1989 a "carnival of revolution."[2]

Garton Ash's quotation gets at the heart one of the most nagging problems of interpreting 1989: if the dominos of revolution in the region had begun to topple a decade earlier, in Poland, why was the world—including the reformers themselves—caught by surprise? Even Garton Ash wrote in his account of 1989, "Why did it happen? And why so quickly? No one in East Germany predicted [the fall of the Wall]."[3] Since 1989, American and European academics have asked why they, too, failed to predict the end of the Cold War. Five years after the revolution, political scientist Henry Steck declared, "The rapid and unexpected collapse of the Communist systems of the Soviet Union and Eastern Europe continues to mystify scholars and citizens alike."[4]

While scholars of Eastern Europe struggle to explain why they had not foreseen revolutionary changes of 1989, many China experts are trying to understand why events there ended in tragedy rather than jubilation. The "Beijing Spring" had begun auspiciously, when students gathered in Tiananmen Square to mourn reformist Communist Party official Hu Yaobang. The movement had grown to include tens of thousands of students, workers, and ordinary citizens from across China, defying the government's orders to disband and resisting martial law for more than a month. On June 4, though, viewers watched with shock and despair as armored vehicles bulldozed the papier-mâché "Goddess of Democracy" and other detritus of aborted revolution, after killing unarmed citizens in order to reach the square.

---

[2] Padraic Kenney, *A Carnival of Revolution* (Princeton, NJ: Princeton University Press, 2002).

[3] Ash, *The Magic Lantern*, 64.

[4] Henry Steck, "Book Review: The Walls Came Tumbling Down: The Collapse of Communism in Eastern Europe by Gale Stokes," *Library Journal*, 118, no. 14 (September, 1993): 206.

The most famous image of China in 1989—one of the most powerful photographs of the twentieth century—is the "Tank Man" photograph taken by Jeff Widener of the Associated Press. Depicting a lone protester blocking a column of People's Liberation Army tanks, it shows determination in the face of an oppressive state, but the gesture is grim. This is a sharp contrast to the celebrations of sledgehammer-wielding Germans atop the Berlin Wall literally tearing down the means of their repression.

Although Eastern Europe and China dominated the headlines as epicenters of revolution and are the focus of this collection, 1989 saw dramatic and unanticipated changes across the globe. In South Africa, a deeply entrenched apartheid government opened negotiations with the long-outlawed African National Congress, eventually leading to the end of the apartheid system. Elections in Latin America lacked the drama of events in Eastern Europe. Citizens and opposition leaders called for transparent governance, democratization, and multiparty elections and pointed to successes in other nations to justify their own goals.

Historian Patrick Manning distinguishes between studying "events" and studying "social processes" in his comparative essay on 1789 and 1989.[5] The events of 1989 are graphic and stunning, but two decades after the events that ended the Cold War, we can better understand the longer processes that made the theater of 1989 possible. This book seeks to understand the global phenomena that caused democracy movements to explode in China and Eastern Europe, and also southern Africa and Latin America. In the short term, Manning points to "widespread distress with the autocratic power of government,"[6] spread by the communication revolution, which itself inspired other dissident groups to use political tactics from successes abroad. These events were unique and unprecedented, but they also represented culminations of longer historical trends, including decolonization and international recognition of ethnic and racial rights, two processes begun after the Second World War.

---

[5] Patrick Manning, "1789–1792 and 1989–1992: Global Interaction of Social Movements," *World History Connections*, 3, no. 1 (October, 2005).

[6] Manning, "1789–1792."

## Antecedents

The most common response to why scholars, dissidents, and politicians expressed shock at the rapid changes 1989 brought was that the Cold War had become "normal." Historian John Lewis Gaddis argued that scholars tend to "bias our historical and theoretical analyses too much toward continuity."[7] Even U.S. President George H. W. Bush cautioned against the reunification of Germany and the breakup of the Soviet Union. Rather than celebrating American victory in the Cold War, he and his leading foreign policy advisors worried that these changes would upset the balance of power and lead to an unstable and dangerous world. Future events would show that these worries were not without cause.

The documents in Part II, Antecedents, demonstrate both the entrenched nature of the Cold War system and cracks in its foundation that were evident almost from its onset. The Yalta Agreement and Winston Churchill's famous "Iron Curtain" speech outlined an understanding that the world would be divided into two spheres of influence: one authoritarian and communist, dominated by the Soviet Union, and one liberal-democratic and capitalist, led by the United States and its Western European allies. The division of the world that Churchill theorized—made concrete several years later by the Berlin Wall—became accepted as a permanent feature of the world order after 1945.

Although the United States experienced internal instability during the Cold War, such as massive protests over civil rights and the Vietnam War, it was the struggles within the Soviet sphere of influence that laid the foundations of the 1989 revolutions. Attempts at internal reform in the Warsaw Pact countries, particularly the 1956 Hungarian Uprising and Czechoslovakia's 1968 Prague Spring, were ended by Soviet-led invasions into supposedly sovereign nations. The tension and disbelief that marked the protest movements in 1989 stemmed largely from the 180-degree turn in Soviet policy, as Soviet Premier Mikhail Gorbachev promised a hands-off approach.

---

[7] John Lewis Gaddis, "International Relations Theory and the End of the Cold War," *International Security*, 17, no. 3 (Winter, 1992–1993): 5–58; 48.

The human rights movements that emerged in the 1970s also contributed to the ever increasing size of the cracks in the Cold War foundation. Especially in Czechoslovakia following the 1968 invasion, dissidents pursued a more cautious approach to change. When Czechoslovakia signed the 1976 Helsinki Accords on human rights, Václav Havel and other dissidents founded Charter 77, reporting abuses, as defined by these accords, to its own government. The Charter Movement focused on free speech, garnering international attention when it defended the banned rock group, Plastic People of the Universe, but the movement remained small and limited in scope, concentrating on the intellectual sector.

In Poland, on the other hand, dissident movements enjoyed broad popular support throughout the Cold War era. In June 1956, workers in Poznan rose up against food and consumer good shortages. While the striking Polish workers did not gain satisfaction on all counts, they did achieve a liberalization of their state and acknowledgment of Polish national traditions, especially Catholicism. In 1978, the election of Krakow Bishop Karol Wojtyła as Pope John Paul II galvanized the Polish population to reach again for economic, political, and cultural changes.

In 1980, the Solidarity movement was born. Following the firing of a popular crane operator known to support workers' rights, the Gdansk shipyards, the center of 1970 uprisings, erupted into a large-scale protest movement. Lech Wałęsa, a former electrician at the shipyards, returned to lead a strike, and dissident intellectual leaders arrived to lend their support. Solidarity, as well as the Polish pope in the Vatican, advocated a nonviolent resolution to the conflicts with the state. The Gdansk agreement of September 1980 recognized the workers' right to strike, and Solidarity became a national movement, rather than a local labor union. Although Poland suffered under martial law and political repression during the 1980s, the reemergence of Solidarity in 1989 sparked the revolutions across the continent.

\* \* \*

In China, the events of 1989 were part of a long tradition of protest that extended in many ways to at least the Ming Dynasty (1368–1644), when scholars protested corruption in government as part of their moral duty, drawing on Confucian teachings that upright officials were obliged to criticize misrule. Even earlier, Mencius—a fourth-century BCE interpreter of Confucius—insisted that the people were justified in overthrowing tyrants. In the twentieth century, student protests that began on May 4, 1919, are generally seen as the start of modern Chinese nationalism. Limiting our scope even more, the antecedents of 1989 begin with the succession to Mao Zedong. Zhou Enlai, China's premier, died in January 1976, as Mao himself was gravely ill. Paranoid, Mao viewed the demonstrations mourning the charismatic and popular Zhou in Tiananmen Square as a personal attack and ordered police to disperse the mourners. Many—no one knows how many—were killed. This "Tiananmen Incident" set a precedent for both the power of an important leader's death and the use of state violence to disperse protesters.

When Mao himself died that October, a power struggle ensued, eventually won by Deng Xiaoping, a veteran revolutionary who envisioned and orchestrated China's opening to the world. By 1979, as Deng toured America to promote China's economic opening, the first signs of political dissent appeared on a wall near the center of Beijing. This "Democracy Wall" included Wei Jingsheng's call for a "Fifth Modernization"—democracy—if China were to become a modern nation (Zhou Enlai had earlier promoted "Four Modernizations" that China needed to embrace: agriculture, industry, technology, and defense). Wei (like Poland's Lech Wałęsa, an electrician) was arrested and imprisoned for voicing his dissent. Although his writings did not inspire a mass movement in China, new voices calling for change continued to rise up. These voices peaked in December 1986, when waves of student protest, mainly in Beijing and Shanghai, called for greater political freedoms. The protests were put down, but they alarmed the government, and those who had encouraged the students were censured. Hu Yaobang, the general secretary of the Communist Party, was removed from power.

From China to Eastern Europe to South Africa, global human rights movements that had been growing since the Second World War had led to increased tensions between citizens and their governments. The year 1989 saw the culmination of decades of conflict and protest, but with results unplanned and unthinkable to either the movements' or the states' leaders.

## The Year 1989

As much as 1989 was a time of new beginnings around the world, it was also a time of farewells. In January, Ronald Reagan completed his second term of office, and in his farewell address, Reagan remarked on the "satisfying new closeness with the Soviet Union."[8] Yet, Reagan's speech did not envision the collapse of the two-superpower system that had dominated his entire political career. Instead, he hoped that the "Soviet Union that eventually emerges from this process is a less threatening one."[9]

In 1989, which marked the Soviets' withdrawal from Afghanistan following a ten-year war, Gorbachev announced his intention to hold limited open elections in the Soviet Union: two-thirds of the 2,250-seat Congress of People's Deputies could be contested by noncommunist candidates. Many dissidents, such as scientist and Nobel Peace Laureate Andrei Sakharov, continued to criticize Gorbachev for not opening all the seats of the Congress and for restricting elections to the more powerful Supreme Soviet. Nonetheless, the elections of 1989 were unprecedented and resulted in the election of several important opposition voices including Sakharov himself, Boris Yeltsin, and historian Roy Medvedev.

In China, the catalyst for movement was the death of Hu Yaobang on April 15. Hu had remained popular among students and intellectuals after his removal in 1987, and many came out to mourn publicly, gathering on the steps of the Monument to Revolutionary Martyrs in Tiananmen Square—just as mourners for Zhou Enlai had gathered in 1976. The monument commemorates all those who died for the cause of revolution in twentieth-century China, and by congregating there the students linked themselves explicitly to a long tradition of protest, one acknowledged and legitimated by the Communist Party. Continuing to draw on the tradition of dissent, on April 22—the day of Hu's fu-

[8] http://www.ronaldreagan.com/sp_21.html.
[9] Ibid.

neral—students knelt on the steps of the Congress hall with a petition for Premier Li Peng. The gesture evoked Confucian officials offering a loyal opposition to a corrupt government. Li, though, refused to accept the petition in person, rejecting the gesture, and angry students responded by boycotting classes and gathering in the square. More than 100,000 people—mainly students—joined the protests.

The occupation of Tiananmen Square became a standoff between the protesters and the Chinese government that neither had sought or anticipated. The leadership on both sides was inconsistent and unclear, as groups with different agendas and different goals jockeyed for position. Time, perhaps, would have helped the two sides reach an understanding, but time was short: on May 15, Mikhail Gorbachev was due to arrive in Beijing for the first visit by a Soviet head of state to China in thirty years. As Gorbachev's visit approached, hard-line and reformist groups battled for the approval of Deng Xiaoping, who still held power despite the lack of any formal title. Zhao Ziyang, the reform-minded general secretary of the Chinese Communist Party (CCP), and Li Peng, the hard-line premier, battled behind the scenes, with Li seeking permission to restore order in the capital through force, while Zhao encouraged press freedom and compromise with the students.

By May 18, after a failed dialogue between Li Peng and student leaders, the hard-liners had won. That evening, Deng Xiaoping gathered his senior government leaders and polled them about imposing martial law; only Zhao Ziyang dissented. At dawn the next morning, Zhao (accompanied by current premier Wen Jiabao, then his chief assistant) appeared with a bullhorn and addressed the students. He apologized to the students, cryptically, for his failures, and urged them to cease the hunger strike and think about the future. He then disappeared from public view (and lived under house arrest until his death in 2005). The government put in motion plans for implementing martial law.[10]

For the next week, Beijing citizens stopped soldiers attempting to reach the square. A last moment of optimism emerged on May 30, as one of the Beijing Spring's most enduring symbols arrived in the

---

[10] Zhao Ziyang's memoirs were smuggled out of China and posthumously published in May 2009 as *Prisoner of the State*, (New York: Simon & Schuster, 2009).

square, the "Goddess of Democracy" statue. The statue's arrival emboldened the students in the square and inspired an international TV audience, with its allusion to American and French revolutionary traditions, but she did not herald success in Tiananmen Square. On June 3, People's Liberation Army (PLA) troops were ordered to take the square "at all costs," and soldiers gunned down citizens blocking their entry to the city. By midnight, they arrived at the square. The total death toll in the crackdown may never be known; estimates range from a dozen to several thousand, with several hundred being the most common figure cited. A desperate latenight negotiation permitted the remaining protesters to leave the square just before dawn on June 4.

The next morning, as hospitals throughout the city treated victims of gunshot wounds inflicted by the soldiers on their way to the square, photographers captured the enduring image of the protests: the lone protester who blocked the path of a row of tanks, and then climbed onto the lead tank to talk with its commander. After climbing down, he was escorted away—it's unknown by whom, or why—and not heard from again. His fate remains unknown; his anonymous bravery remains a symbol both of the Beijing Spring and of the challenges and possibilities of speaking truth to power.

\* \* \*

According to Padraic Kenney, many Poles remember the June 4 events in China more vividly than the elections in their own country the same day. In Wroclaw, a memorial to the victims of Tiananmen Square, which featured parts of a Soviet tank and a mangled bicycle, was bulldozed within a day. Poles, Hungarians, and Czechoslovakians created shrines of flowers and candles. As Kenney explained, "The fear that such a thing could have happened to them was very real."[11]

Worsening economic conditions and workers' protests had made clear to the Polish government that negotiations with the opposition were unavoidable. "Roundtable" negotiations between Solidarity and the state began in February 1989, and Solidarity was officially legalized in April, just as the Chinese students were occupying Tiananmen Square. Despite institutional "guarantees" that the

---

[11] Kenney, *A Carnival of Revolution*, 257–58.

Communist Party would maintain a majority, Solidarity took all 161 of the open seats in the lower house of the legislature and 99 of the 100 Senate seats in the June 4 elections. The overwhelming majority in the lower house meant that the Senate could block legislation sponsored by the communist majority in the upper house.

While the Poles were celebrating but also watching the tumultuous events in Beijing, the Hungarians were watching the Poles. Inspired by the changes in the Soviet Union and Poland, the Hungarian Communist Party created a "revolution from within."[12] Whereas in Poland—and elsewhere in the region later that year—a single bloc of anticommunist resistance emerged, in Hungary a plethora of small, narrowly defined political organizations appeared. This enabled true multiparty elections in March 1990 but also made the transition to a new system more complex. On October 7, 1989, the Hungarian Communist Party, at a special Party Congress, voted itself out of existence.

As Hungary liberalized, it began dismantling the barbed wire fences that divided Hungary from Austria, or "the West." While in years past, the Hungarian state helped restrict East German visits to the West German Embassy in Budapest, the government was no longer willing to aid their ally in keeping the East German population in the East. In a complete reversal of policy, the Hungarian state even set up refugee camps for East Germans. By September, when East German Party Secretary Erich Honecker banned all travel to Hungary, 50,000 refugees had made their way to Austria, West Germany, or Czechoslovakia, where they hoped to visit the West European embassy. A popular joke that summer was of a sign posted on the border: "East Germany: Would the last person please turn off the lights?"[13]

As in China, a visit by Mikhail Gorbachev catalyzed events. Gorbachev attended the ceremonies marking the fortieth anniversary of the East German state in October 1989, and he was greeted with enthusiasm from the Berlin crowds chanting "Gorby! Gorby!" In his speech, Gorbachev called for solutions to the problems facing

---

[12] Patrick H. O'Neil, "Revolution from Within: Analysis, Transitions from Authoritarianism, and the Case of Hungary," *World Politics*, 48, no. 4 (1996): 579–603.

[13] Quoted from Jeffrey B. Symynkywicz, *1989: The Year the World Changed* (Parsippany, NJ: Dillon Press, 1996), 74.

Eastern Europe, which could only be solved through modernization.[14] He reiterated earlier guarantees that the Soviet Union
would no longer interfere with domestic matters in the Warsaw
Bloc. "First, I should tell our Western partners that matters relating
to the German Democratic Republic are decided not in Moscow,
but in Berlin"[15]

International media attention focused on Berlin, but the real
political action was in Leipzig, where weekly demonstrations grew
to record numbers through September. The slogan of the Leipzigers
was "We are the People," playing on the idea that the "people's
republic" did not truly represent the ordinary citizens. By October
16, the crowd had swelled to over 100,000. Reportedly, Honecker
authorized the use of force against the demonstrators, but Egon
Krenz, national chief of security, refused to carry out the orders.
With the party leadership losing faith in Honecker, he was forced to
resign on October 18. Demonstrations spread throughout East
Germany, culminating in a half million people filling the East
Berlin streets by early November. Meanwhile, the Czechoslovak
government opened its border to East Germans wishing to flee the
chaos, and 50,000 entered the neighboring state. By November 7,
the East German cabinet felt it had no choice but to resign.

Two days later, after returning from a family vacation, Minister
of Press and Information Günter Schabowski was thrust into a
press conference with the national and international media. The
transcripts of the conference depict the chaotic and rapid nature of
events in 1989. Schabowski, somewhat accidentally, announced
that the border between East and West Germany would open, "effective immediately." The news spread rapidly throughout Berlin
and residents on both sides of the hated barrier rushed to the Wall.
The scenes of that night are among the most vivid and powerful of
the year: East German Trabants—a plastic-bodied car that symbol-
ized East German industrial failure—lining up to pass through
the Brandenburg Gate; young Germans embracing on top of
the Wall.

---

[14] Open Society archives. http://files.osa.ceu.hu/holdings/300/8/3/text/120-4-61.shtml.

[15] Serge Schmemann, "Gorbachev Lends Honecker a Hand," *New York Times*, October 7,
1989.

The regimes that fell at the *end* of 1989—Czechoslovakia, Bulgaria, and Romania—were considered the least likely to change at all. In the end, though, they fell the fastest and hardest. In Prague, university students gathered on November 17 to mark the fiftieth anniversary of student protests against the Nazi occupation. In 1989, though, student leaders who had recently created a self-government moved beyond the traditional anti-fascist rhetoric and decided to write an appeal to the government. In response, police blocked the student procession and beat several protesters. An un-founded rumor that one student had been killed spread throughout the country and galvanized support for the student movement.

Within days, the Civic Forum—a broad coalition of dissidents from intellectual, student, and religious circles, with Václav Havel at its center—had been formed; in Slovakia its equivalent, Public against Violence, emerged. The police could no longer hold back demonstrators from entering Prague's largest square, Wenceslas Square. Students gathered at the memorial to "Good King Wenceslas," the patron saint and founder of the Bohemian Kingdom. By midweek, when Havel addressed the crowd, half a million demonstrators were camped on the historic square. On November 27—Garton Ash's now-famous "tenth day"—a general strike shut down the country. The party belatedly offered a coali-tion power-sharing government to the dissident leaders, but the revolution had gone too far. By the end of the month, the still-communist legislature selected Havel as the nation's first noncom-munist president in forty-one years.

Quieter changes were taking place elsewhere. In Bulgaria, a peaceful demonstration on the day Sofians received the news about the Berlin Wall convinced seventy-eight-year-old communist leader Todor Zhivkov, who had led Bulgaria for over three decades, to step down. Outside of Europe, movements for democracy and increased human rights were also spreading. On September 20, F. W. de Klerk was inaugurated president of South Africa after the stroke and resignation of apartheid hard-liner P. W. Botha earlier that year. In his inaugural address, de Klerk announced the upcoming release of political prisoners, must notably Nelson Mandela, who would leave his twenty-seven-year prison term on Robben Island in February 1990. De Klerk also promised to begin negotiations on an end to apartheid, a harsh system of racial segregation legally enforced in the country since 1948. In November and December, elections took place in Chile and Brazil for the first time in decades. Manuel Noriega of Panama was forcibly removed from power by a U.S. military invasion. Although most of the attention in 1989 was on the communist world, the United States too was learning from the events of the year. No longer was the simplistic division of the world into two spheres of influence able to maintain a safe, stable peace.

A remarkable aspect of 1989 was the peaceful means to change chosen by the vast majority of dissidents, as well as the restraint shown by most governments—China being the glaring exception—in dealing with the large-scale demonstrations. As Padraic Kenney remarked, most events in 1989 were "velvet,"[16] using the label given to the swift and peaceful revolution in Czechoslovakia. The year would not end that way, though. In Romania, the harshest regime in East Central Europe, the dictatorship fell violently.

Nicolae Ceauşescu came to power in Romania in 1965 and ruled as an eccentric and brutal dictator for more than three decades. As 1989 neared its end, so did Ceauşescu's rule. On December 18, following months of unrest, thousands of Romanians flooded the capital demanding Ceauşescu's resignation. The Ceauşescus escaped to their estate via helicopter but were later captured and brought to a military headquarters in Tirgoviste. A "kangaroo trial"[17] in front of a military tribunal lasted nine hours. Excerpts of the transcript demonstrate the Ceauşescus' clear separation from reality. The final image of the revolutions of 1989 was the bloody, bullet-sprayed bodies of Nicolae and Elena Ceauşescu, executed on Christmas Day.

## Aftermath

Political philosopher and economist Francis Fukuyama theorized that 1989 represented "the end of history" in his essay of the same title. Fukuyama's thesis (which he has since amended)

---

[16] Kenney, *A Carnival of Revolution.*

[17] Gale Stokes, *The Walls Came Tumbling Down: The Collapse of Communism in Eastern Europe* (New York: Oxford University Press, 1993), 166.

contended that the fall of communism concluded the clash of ideologies that had defined human history for centuries and that economic and political liberalism would now dominate human
societies.

Fukuyama's thesis—which was first published in the summer of
1989—seemed borne out by the events of that autumn. All of the
communist governments in East Central Europe established in the
wake of World War II (except Albania's, which fell in 1992), collapsed in the last half of 1989. The Soviet Union, which had
spawned them, was itself moving toward disintegration. Inflation
and fiscal uncertainty marked the new capitalist system, but the
economies in the region grew steadily. Most citizens were willing to
add risk to their economic lives in return for an increased freedom
in political decisions and foreign travel. Yet an integrated Europe
faced serious issues. François Furet, a French historian, worried that
a West European culture of individual wealth and selfishness would
bleed into the new Central European members of the European
Union (EU). Furet expressed concern that without stronger
European institutions and a willingness for citizen engagement in
civil society, European leadership would fail to manage crises such
as the war in Yugoslavia or the growing immigrant population in
Europe.[18]

The revolutions of 1989 were not panaceas: new problems appeared, and many old problems, particularly the ethnic and religious tensions that had been suppressed or ignored during years of
authoritarian rule, reemerged. As early as January 1, 1990, Václav
Havel told his new constituency, "Our country is not flourishing."
He discussed a "contaminated" ecological and moral landscape in
Czechoslovakia and warned about the outmoded economy and
poor educational system. He also pointed to the rise of nationalism,
asking his fellow Czechoslovaks to think of the country as made up
of two nations as well as national minorities and to see that citizens
were obligated to respect one another's traditions and culture.
Three years after Havel's historic speech, his country peacefully
broke into the Czech and Slovak Republics.

---

[18] François Furet, "Europe after Utopianism," *Journal of Democracy*, 6, no. 1 (1995): 79–89.

Czechoslovakia's "Velvet Divorce" did not have a peaceful corollary in Yugoslavia. There the country erupted into civil war, genocide, and political turmoil. Yugoslavia did not experience the dramatic revolution of 1989. Its journey from communism to nationalism had begun with the death of Marshall Tito in 1980. Tito had fought long-standing national mistrust, particularly between Croats and Serbs, by forging a Yugoslav identity and putting down displays of individual religious or nationalist culture. In 1987, Slobodan Milosevic rose to political prominence with a rousing nationalistic speech in Kosovo telling the local Serb population to stay in the region and that "No one will ever beat a Serb again."[19] In June 1989, on the 600th anniversary of the battle of Kosovo Polje, when the Ottoman Empire defeated the Serbs, Milosevic followed up his earlier speech with more nationalist rhetoric. Milosevic's Serbian nationalism combined with Croatia and Slovenia's determination for more autonomy led to a bloody civil war. In Bosnia-Herzegovina, "ethnic cleansing" targeted the country's Muslim population.

Yugoslavia's demise reflected the most extreme and violent example of nationalism in Eastern Europe, but it was not the only one. Throughout the region, nationalist rhetoric was used against minorities. Most egregiously, the Roma (gypsy) populations were often victims of attacks, discrimination, or neglect. Zoltan Barany has called the Roma peoples of East Central Europe "the orphans of transition."[20] The rapid economic changes in the region also highlighted disparities among ethnic groups and brewed resentment toward those in the more prosperous regions.

As nationalism surged in Eastern Europe, a simultaneous call for reintegration into Europe emerged. Several of the post-communist states joined NATO in 1999 and the EU in 2004. For many, these achievements signaled the true end to the communist period and the victory of the revolutions of 1989. However, others in the region, like Czech President Václav Klaus, warned that again the

---

[19] Stokes, *The Walls Came Tumbling Down*, 233.

[20] Zoltan Barany, "Orphans of Transition: Gypsies in Eastern Europe," *Journal of Democracy*, 9, no. 3 (1998): 142–56.

small Central European nations could be swallowed up by their larger, more powerful neighbors.

Nationalism played a key role in the dissolution of the Soviet Empire, with the Baltic Republics and Georgia leading multiple campaigns for sovereignty. Gorbachev's reforms, embraced and celebrated in the West, met growing skepticism in his own country. Dissidents believed the reforms did not go far enough in taking the economy and political system in a new direction, whereas hard-line Marxists in the party were angered by Gorbachev's "watered down" communism.

Economic and social concerns dominated politics after 1989. Few envisioned—or even desired—the rapid marketization of the economy. The fast-paced economic changes benefited many younger, educated urbanites, while other sectors of society suffered both economic and social setbacks. For example, retired citizens found that their pensions could not keep up with the rapid inflation brought on by the new economic systems. Women were faced with unexpected difficulties as state-run day care facilities closed and the quotas set aside for women were abolished in some government and career sectors. In East Germany and Poland, women also struggled with changes to the very liberal abortion laws they had become accustomed to. While many women celebrated the increased availability of contraceptives and feminine hygiene products, they also realized that cultural and economic transformation in their countries would bring unexpected changes to their reproductive lives. Industrial workers faced layoffs and unfamiliar practices when their places of employment were privatized, often by foreign firms.

In China, by contrast, the Communist Party did not fall. Military force had kept the government in power, but analysts gave numerous reasons why the CCP would be unable to govern in the wake of 1989: events in Eastern Europe had discredited communism as a viable ideology; by ordering troops to fire on unarmed protesters, the government—which claimed to represent the people—had forfeited its legitimacy. Predictions ranged from a gradual weakening of the communist regime to popular revolt to regional disintegration. To the contrary, though, the CCP was able to use strong central planning to accelerate economic growth and promote nationalism, positioning itself as the leader of China's rise to global prominence, and it grew stronger over the following decades.

The Chinese government cemented its power after 1989 by taking three lessons from the events in Eastern Europe. First, the CCP concluded that political compromise and accommodation had led to the downfall of communist governments. European communist parties had included a broader array of political voices in the government in order to co-opt dissent and prevent mass revolutions. The events of 1989 showed this policy to be a failure, and the CCP became more determined than ever to maintain its monopoly on political power. The second lesson the CCP took from Eastern Europe was that economic deprivation and a lack of consumer goods had motivated people to take political action. Although intellectuals might question a government's right to rule, few people, the CCP reasoned, would actively oppose a government that was meeting their material needs and providing a standard of living that was acceptable and improving. The CCP thus focused China's economic growth on enriching and expanding the middle class and making consumer comforts widely affordable. In the years following 1989, political dissent in China appeared to fade, as China's youth traded political freedom for economic opportunity.

The third lesson the Chinese Communist Party took from events in Eastern Europe was the tremendous power of nationalism. In Europe, nationalism had asserted itself after the fall of communism, tearing apart (and reunifying) states and prompting bloody wars. In China, the CCP promoted nationalism as a means of maintaining its rule in the absence of ideology. China's leaders had abandoned the traditional ideological foundation of socialism, introducing reforms that led to greater economic inequality and unraveled the social safety net. To replace the ideological commitment to equality, the government promoted itself as the creator of a strong Chinese nation, eager to gain a place as a global power.

The fall of communism in East Central Europe and the Soviet Union had ripple effects around the globe. In South Africa, the reasons for the dismantling of the apartheid system were manifold. Political unrest made much of the country unmanageable; the economy struggled against internal labor troubles as well as international sanctions and boycotts. The end of the Cold War also removed a major argument of the white government: that apartheid—by maintaining stability in South Africa—protected southern Africa from the expansion of communism. The African National Congress had a strong Marxist contingency and backing from the Soviet Union. During the late 1980s, the Soviet Union and the United States actually worked together to convince South Africa to end its military occupation of Namibia, which finally received independence in March 1990. The joint efforts of the two superpowers in the Namibia conflict demonstrated that the Cold War divisions were weakening and that the two sides could cooperate across their ideological divisions.

## The Difference a Year Made

A year is an arbitrary unit of time, defined by the earth's orbit of the sun. It would be foolish to suggest that a single year represents a sudden and fundamental shift in human history or that all the causes and results of that change can be contained in any span of 365 days. Of course, the events of 1989 are part of processes that began much earlier and continue even today. Yet the spectacular and far-reaching events of 1989 cannot be dismissed as coincidence. On every continent, in dozens of countries, people reassessed the dynamics of power between governments and their citizens. In many cases, long-standing and seemingly permanent power relationships evaporated almost overnight. In others, fears of government reprisal proved well-founded.

Certain themes are apparent. The value of civil society in governance was central to almost all the protesters' demands. Ideology—most often communism, but also apartheid and fascism—was in decline. Another important question scholars grapple with is the role of the United States and the Soviet Union—as leaders of the Cold War superpowers in a bipolar world—versus the grassroots activism of the citizenry. Because 1989 ended with the fall of communism in Eastern Europe, Reagan is often perceived as the victor. Reagan, though, was not merely a Cold Warrior, and his views moderated over the course of his second term in office, which coincided with Gorbachev's first years as head of the Soviet Communist Party. Gorbachev instituted two policies: *perestroika* (rebuilding) and *glasnost* (openness). Perestroika proposed modernization and movement away from the command economy of the Soviet Union. Glasnost represented a plan to combat corruption in the party and to introduce gradually freedoms in speech and the press. Padraic Kenney has reminded us that the grassroots campaigns among intellectuals, church members, environmentalists, artists, students, and others were well under way throughout the region before Gorbachev took office.[21] Most scholars now attribute a limited role to both Gorbachev and Reagan in the revolutions of 1989, but the international media loved to spotlight the two charismatic figures, and their speeches and summits created a stable backdrop to the "carnival" of demonstrations throughout the region.

The bipolar world of the Cold War—in creation since World War I and dominant since World War II—ended in 1989. Only one superpower remained, but hopes that this would usher in an era of "Pax Americana" quickly faded, as smaller conflicts (in Iraq, Somalia, and the Balkans, for instance) were no longer proxy wars but were just as deadly and no less intractable. By September 11, 2001, it was clear that the post–Cold War world was not safer than the one it replaced. Indeed, the American "victors" in the Cold War found themselves facing daily security alerts and levels of fear that the Cold War had not produced in forty years.

The year 1989 was not the end of history. In almost every country in the world, however, New Year's Day, 1990, was remarkably different from January 1, 1989. The intervening 365 days had indeed changed the world. The Cold War and apartheid had suffered mortal blows, as had the illusion that China's dramatic economic rise would be accompanied by an easy transition to Western-style democracy. With so many fundamental changes under way, we can say that 1989 was the end of the twentieth century.

---

[21] Kenney, *A Carnival of Revolution*, especially 121–23.

# 1989 Chronologies

## China

April 15: Death of former Chinese Communist Party (CCP) Secretary-General Hu Yaobang.

April 17: About 2,000 Beijing University students march to Tiananmen Square, beginning occupation of the square that lasts continuously until June 4.

April 22: Funeral of Hu Yaobang. Simultaneous demonstration in Tiananmen Square.

April 26: *People's Daily* editorial condemning the student protests as a conspiracy to promote "turmoil."

April 27: First major street demonstrations. About 100,000 students march to the square in protest of the editorial.

May 4: Anniversary of 1919 student demonstrations against Western imperialism and weakness in the Chinese government. Major street demonstrations.

May 13: Hunger strike in Tiananmen Square begins.

May 14: "Dialogue" meeting between student protesters (including Wu'er Kaixi) and Premier Li Peng.

May 15: Soviet President Mikhail Gorbachev arrives in Beijing. Ceremonies planned for Tiananmen Square are canceled or moved because of the ongoing protests.

May 17: More than one million protesters march in support of hunger strikers. Deng Xiaoping rejects Zhao Ziyang's plea for restraint.

May 19: Martial law declared; first army attempt to occupy Beijing.

May 29: Goddess of Democracy statue erected in Tiananmen Square.

June 3: Second army attempt to occupy Beijing; army opens fire.

June 4: Army takes control of Tiananmen Square.

## Eastern Europe

February 6: Roundtable talks in Poland return Solidarity union to legal status.

May 2: Border between Austria and Hungary opened.

June 4: Polish elections, Solidarity victory.

June 28: Milosevic speech at Kosovo Field.

September 12: Mazowiecki forms noncommunist government in Poland.

October 7: Fortieth anniversary of East Germany; Gorbachev visits Berlin.

October 18: Eric Honecker resigns as president of East Germany.

October 23: Hungary declares itself a democratic republic, plans multiparty elections.

November 9: Berlin Wall falls.

November 10: Bulgarian president and party leader Todor Zhivkov resigns.

November 17: Prague Revolution begins with demonstrations in Wenceslas Square.

December 10: Czechoslovak president Gustav Husák resigns.

December 16: Timisoara protests begin Romanian revolution.

December 22: Brandenburg Gate reopens in Berlin.

December 25: Romanian dictator Nicolae Ceauşescu and his wife executed.

December 29: Federal Assembly elects Václav Havel president of Czechoslovakia.

# Part II
## Antecedents

### Cold War

## Yalta Agreement (1945)

*In February 1945, the "Big Three" of Roosevelt, Churchill, and Stalin, met at Yalta, the Crimean resort on the Black Sea. Many historians regard the meeting as the beginning of the Cold War. In return for the promise of the Soviet Union's aid in the war with Japan, Roosevelt and Churchill made several concessions to Stalin, regarding a Soviet sphere of influence in Eastern Europe. Important issues discussed at the conference included the dismemberment and occupation of Germany, the future structure of a United Nations, and the status of Poland. Excerpts of the agreement are presented here.*

### Protocol of Proceedings of Crimea Conference

The Crimea Conference of the heads of the Governments of the United States of America, the United Kingdom, and the Union of Soviet Socialist Republics, which took place from Feb. 4 to 11, came to the following conclusions:

*I. World Organization*

It was decided:

1. That a United Nations conference on the proposed world organization should be summoned for Wednesday, 25 April, 1945, and should be held in the United States of America.

23

2. The nations to be invited to this conference should be:
   (a) the United Nations as they existed on 8 Feb., 1945; and
   (b) Such of the Associated Nations as have declared war on the common enemy by 1 March, 1945. (For this purpose, by the term "Associated Nations" was meant the eight Associated Nations and Turkey.) When the conference on world organization is held, the delegates of the United Kingdom and United State[s] of America will support a proposal to admit to original membership two Soviet Socialist Republics, i.e., the Ukraine and White Russia.

3. That the United States Government, on behalf of the three powers, should consult the Government of China and the French Provisional Government in regard to decisions taken at the present conference concerning the proposed world organization.

4. That the text of the invitation to be issued to all the nations which would take part in the United Nations conference should be as follows:
   "The Government of the United States of America, on behalf of itself and of the Governments of the United Kingdom, the Union of Soviet Socialistic Republics and the Republic of China and of the Provisional Government of the French Republic invite the Government of ———— to send representatives to a conference to be held on 25 April, 1945, or soon thereafter, at San Francisco, in the United States of America, to prepare a charter for a general international organization for the maintenance of international peace and security.
   "The above-named Governments suggest that the conference consider as affording a basis for such a Charter the proposals for the establishment of a general international organization which were made public last October as a result of the Dumbarton Oaks conference and which have now been supplemented by the following provisions for Section C of Chapter VI:
   C. Voting
   "1. Each member of the Security Council should have one vote.
   "2. Decisions of the Security Council on procedural matters should be made by an affirmative vote of seven members.

"3. Decisions of the Security Council on all matters should be made by an affirmative vote of seven members, including the concurring votes of the permanent members; provided that, in decisions under Chapter VIII, Section A and under the second sentence of Paragraph 1 of Chapter VIII, Section C, a party to a dispute should abstain from voting.

"Further information as to arrangements will be transmitted subsequently.

"In the event that the Government of ———— desires in advance of the coherence to present views or comments concerning the proposals, the Government of the United States of America will be pleased to transmit such views and comments to the other participating Governments."

Territorial trusteeship:

It was agreed that the five nations which will have permanent seats on the Security Council should consult each other prior to the United Nations conference on the question of territorial trusteeship.

The acceptance of this recommendation is subject to its being made clear that territorial trusteeship will only apply to

(a) existing mandates of the League of Nations; (b) territories detached from the enemy as a result of the present war; (c) any other territory which might voluntarily be placed under trusteeship; and (d) no discussion of actual territories is contemplated at the forthcoming United Nations conference or in the preliminary consultations, and it will be a matter for subsequent agreement which territories within the above categories will be place[d] under trusteeship.

[Begin first section published Feb., 13, 1945.]

## II. Declaration of Liberated Europe

The following declaration has been approved:

The Premier of the Union of Soviet Socialist Republics, the Prime Minister of the United Kingdom and the President of the United States of America have consulted with each other in the common interests of the people of their countries and those of liberated Europe. They jointly declare their mutual agreement to concert during the temporary period of instability in liberated Europe the policies of their three Governments in assisting the peoples liberated from the domination of Nazi Germany and the peoples of the former Axis satellite states of Europe to solve by democratic means their pressing political and economic problems.

The establishment of order in Europe and the rebuilding of national economic life must be achieved by processes which will enable the liberated peoples to destroy the last vestiges of nazism and fascism and to create democratic institutions of their own choice. This is a principle of the Atlantic Charter—the right of all people to choose the form of government under which they will live—the restoration of sovereign rights and self-government to those peoples who have been forcibly deprived to them by the aggressor nations.

To foster the conditions in which the liberated people may exercise these rights, the three governments will jointly assist the people in any European liberated state or former Axis state in Europe where, in their judgment conditions require,

(a) to establish conditions of internal peace; (b) to carry out emergency relief measures for the relief of distressed peoples; (c) to form interim governmental authorities broadly representative of all democratic elements in the population and pledged to the earliest possible establishment through free elections of Governments responsive to the will of the people; and (d) to facilitate where necessary the holding of such elections.

The three Governments will consult the other United Nations and provisional authorities or other Governments in Europe when matters of direct interest to them are under consideration.

When, in the opinion of the three Governments, conditions in any European liberated state or former Axis satellite in Europe make such action necessary, they will immediately consult together on the measure necessary to discharge the joint responsibilities set forth in this declaration.

By this declaration we reaffirm our faith in the principles of the Atlantic Charter, our pledge in the Declaration by the United Nations and our determination to build in cooperation with other peace-loving nations world order, under law, dedicated to peace, security, freedom and general well-being of all mankind.

In issuing this declaration, the three powers express the hope that the Provisional Government of the French Republic may be associated with them in the procedure suggested.

[End first section published February, 13, 1945.]

### III. Dismemberment of Germany

It was agreed that Article 12 (a) of the Surrender terms for Germany should be amended to read as follows:

"The United Kingdom, the United States of America and the Union of Soviet Socialist Republics shall possess supreme authority with respect to Germany. In the exercise of such authority they will take such steps, including the complete dismemberment of Germany as they deem requisite for future peace and security."

The study of the procedure of the dismemberment of Germany was referred to a committee consisting of Mr. Anthony Eden, Mr. John Winant, and Mr. Fedor T. Gusev. This body would consider the desirability of associating with it a French representative.

### IV. Zone of Occupation for the French and Control Council for Germany

It was agreed that a zone in Germany, to be occupied by the French forces, should be allocated France. This zone would be formed out of the British and American zones and its extent would be settled by the British and Americans in consultation with the French Provisional Government.

It was also agreed that the French Provisional Government should be invited to become a member of the Allied Control Council for Germany.

### V. Reparation

The following protocol has been approved:

Protocol

On the Talks Between the Heads of Three Governments at the Crimean Conference on the Question of the German Reparations in Kind

1. Germany must pay in kind for the losses caused by her to the Allied nations in the course of the war. Reparations are to be

received in the first instance by those countries which have borne the main burden of the war have suffered the heaviest losses and have organized victory over the enemy.

2. Reparation in kind is to be exacted from Germany in three following forms:

   (a) Removals within two years from the surrender of Germany or the cessation of organized resistance from the national wealth of Germany located on the territory of Germany herself as well as outside her territory (equipment, machine tools, ships, rolling stock, German investments abroad, shares of industrial, transport and other enterprises in Germany, etc.), these removals to be carried out chiefly for the purpose of destroying the war potential of Germany. (b) Annual deliveries of goods from current production for a period to be fixed. (c) Use of German labor.

3. For the working out on the above principles of a detailed plan for exaction of reparation from Germany an Allied reparation commission will be set up in Moscow. It will consist of three representatives—one from the Union of Soviet Socialist Republics, one from the United Kingdom and one from the United States of America.

4. With regard to the fixing of the total sum of the reparation as well as the distribution of it among the countries which suffered from the German aggression, the Soviet and American delegations agreed as follows:

"The Moscow reparation commission should take in its initial studies as a basis for discussion the suggestion of the Soviet Government that the total sum of the reparation in accordance with the points (a) and (b) of the Paragraph 2 should be 22 billion dollars and that 50 per cent should go to the Union of Soviet Socialist Republics."

The British delegation was of the opinion that, pending consideration of the reparation question by the Moscow reparation commission, no figures of reparation should be mentioned.

The above Soviet-American proposal has been passed to the Moscow reparation commission as one of the proposals to be considered by the commission.

*VI. Major War Criminals*

The conference agreed that the question of the major war criminals should be the subject of inquiry by the three Foreign Secretaries for report in due course after the close of the conference.

[Begin second section published February 13, 1945.]


*VII. Poland*

The following declaration on Poland was agreed by the conference:

"A new situation has been created in Poland as a result of her complete liberation by the Red Army. This calls for the establishment of a Polish Provisional Government which can be more broadly based than was possible before the recent liberation of the western part of Poland. The Provisional Government which is now functioning in Poland should therefore be reorganized on a broader democratic basis with the inclusion of democratic leaders from Poland itself and from Poles abroad. This new Government should then be called the Polish Provisional Government of National Unity.

"M. Molotov, Mr. Harriman and Sir A. Clark Kerr are authorized as a commission to consult in the first instance in Moscow with members of the present Provisional Government and with other Polish democratic leaders from within Poland and from abroad, with a view to the reorganization of the present Government along the above lines. This Polish Provisional Government of National Unity shall be pledged to the holding of free and unfettered elections as soon as possible on the basis of universal suffrage and secret ballot. In these elections all democratic and anti-Nazi parties shall have the right to take part and to put forward candidates.

"When a Polish Provisional Government [of] National Unity has been properly formed in conformity with the above, the Government of the U.S.S.R., which now maintains diplomatic relations with the present Provisional Government of Poland, and the Government of the United Kingdom and the Government of the United States of America will establish diplomatic relations with the new Polish Provisional Government [of] National Unity, and will exchange

Ambassadors by whose reports the respective Governments will be kept informed about the situation in Poland.

"The three heads of Government consider that the eastern frontier of Poland should follow the Curzon Line with digressions from it in some regions of five to eight kilometers in favor of Poland. They recognize that Poland must receive substantial accessions in territory in the north and west. They feel that the opinion of the new Polish Provisional Government of National Unity should be sought in due course of the extent of these accessions and that the final delimitation of the western frontier of Poland should thereafter await the peace conference."

## VIII. *Yugoslavia*

It was agreed to recommend to Marshal Tito and to Dr. Ivan Subasitch:

(a) That the Tito-Subasitch agreement should immediately be put into effect and a new government formed on the basis of the agreement. (b) That as soon as the new Government has been formed it should declare: (I) That the Anti-Fascist Assembly of the National Liberation (AVNOJ) will be extended to include members of the last Yugoslav Skupstina who have not compromised themselves by collaboration with the enemy, thus forming a body to be known as a temporary Parliament and (II) That legislative acts passed by the Anti-Fascist Assembly of the National Liberation (AVNOJ) will be subject to subsequent ratification by a Constituent Assembly; and that this statement should be published in the communiqué of the conference.

## IX. *Italo-Yugoslav Frontier—Italo-Austrian Frontier*

Notes on these subjects were put in by the British delegation and the American and Soviet delegations agreed to consider them and give their views later.

## X. *Yugoslav-Bulgarian Relations*

There was an exchange of views between the Foreign Secretaries on the question of the desirability of a Yugoslav-Bulgarian pact of alliance. The question at issue was whether a state still under an armistice regime could be allowed to enter into a treaty with another state. Mr. Eden suggested that the Bulgarian and Yugoslav Governments should be informed that this could not be approved. Mr. Stettinius suggested that the British and American Ambassadors should discuss the matter further with Mr. Molotov in Moscow. Mr. Molotov agreed with the proposal of Mr. Stettinius.

## XI. Southeastern Europe

The British delegation put in notes for the consideration of their colleagues on the following subjects:

(a) The Control Commission in Bulgaria. (b) Greek claims upon Bulgaria, more particularly with reference to reparations. (c) Oil equipment in Rumania.

## XII. Iran

Mr. Eden, Mr. Stettinius and Mr. Molotov exchanged views on the situation in Iran. It was agreed that this matter should be pursued through the diplomatic channel.

[Begin third section published February 13, 1945.]

## XIII. Meetings of the Three Foreign Secretaries

The conference agreed that permanent machinery should be set up for consultation between the three Foreign Secretaries; they should meet as often as necessary, probably about every three or four months.

These meetings will be held in rotation in the three capitals, the first meeting being held in London.

[End third section published February 13, 1945.]

## XIV. The Montreaux Convention and the Straits

It was agreed that at the next meeting of the three Foreign Secretaries to be held in London, they should consider proposals which it was understood the Soviet Government would put forward in relation to the Montreaux Convention, and report to their

Governments. The Turkish Government should be informed at the appropriate moment. The forgoing protocol was approved and signed by the three Foreign Secretaries at the Crimean Conference February 11, 1945.

E. R. Stettinius Jr. M. Molotov Anthony Eden


*Agreement Regarding Japan*

The leaders of the three great powers—the Soviet Union, the United States of America and Great Britain—have agreed that in two or three months after Germany has surrendered and the war in Europe is terminated, the Soviet Union shall enter into war against Japan on the side of the Allies on condition that:

1. The status quo in Outer Mongolia (the Mongolian People's Republic) shall be preserved.
2. The former rights of Russia violated by the treacherous attack of Japan in 1904 shall be restored, viz.: (a) The southern part of Sakhalin as well as the islands adjacent to it shall be returned to the Soviet Union; (b) The commercial port of Dairen shall be internationalized, the pre-eminent interests of the Soviet Union in this port being safeguarded, and the lease of Port Arthur as a naval base of the U.S.S.R. restored; (c) The Chinese-Eastern Railroad and the South Manchurian Railroad, which provide an outlet to Dairen, shall be jointly operated by the establishment of a joint Soviet-Chinese company, it being understood that the preeminent interests of the Soviet Union shall be safeguarded and that China shall retain sovereignty in Manchuria;
3. The Kurile Islands shall be handed over to the Soviet Union.

It is understood that the agreement concerning Outer Mongolia and the ports and railroads referred to above will require concurrence of Generalissimo Chiang Kai-shek. The President will take measures in order to maintain this concurrence on advice from Marshal Stalin.

The heads of the three great powers have agreed that these claims of the Soviet Union shall be unquestionably fulfilled after Japan has been defeated.

For its part, the Soviet Union expresses it readiness to conclude with the National Government of China a pact of friendship and

alliance between the U.S.S.R. and China in order to render assistance to China with its armed forces for the purpose of liberating China from the Japanese yoke.

(signed) Joseph Stalin
Franklin D. Roosevelt
Winston S. Churchill
February 11, 1945.

A Decade of American Foreign Policy: Basic Documents, 1941–49. Prepared at the request of the Senate Committee on Foreign Relations by the Staff of the Committee and the Department of State. Washington, DC: Government Printing Office, 1950. Available at http://www.cnn.com/SPECIALS/cold.war/episodes/01/documents/yalta.html.

## DISCUSSION QUESTIONS
1. What steps did the "Big Three" take to ensure the peace following World War II?
2. In what ways did the Yalta Agreement sow the seeds of future conflicts?

# Winston Churchill's Iron Curtain Speech (March 5, 1946)

*Winston Churchill's famous speech at Westminster College in Fulton, Missouri, popularized the phrase "Iron Curtain," a symbolic division between the communist states under growing Soviet influence in East-Central Europe and the liberal democracies of Western Europe. Although the term had appeared in print following the Russian Revolution, Churchill's rhetoric made it the most common metaphor for the Cold War. Some initially criticized Churchill's comments as provocative. The speech was given less than a year after the end of the Second World War, before many of the communist governments took hold in East-Central Europe. Excerpts are presented here.*

The United States stands at this time at the pinnacle of world power. It is a solemn moment for the American democracy. For with this primacy in power is also joined an awe-inspiring accountability to the future. As you look around you, you must feel not only the sense of duty done, but also you must feel anxiety lest you fall below the level of achievement. Opportunity is here now, clear and shining, for both our countries. To reject it or ignore it or fritter it away will bring upon us all the long reproaches of the aftertime.

It is necessary that constancy of mind, persistency of purpose, and the grand simplicity of decision shall rule and guide the conduct of the English-speaking peoples in peace as they did in war. We must, and I believe we shall, provide ourselves equal to this severe requirement.

I have a strong admiration and regard for the valiant Russian people and for my wartime comrade, Marshal Stalin. There is deep sympathy and goodwill in Britain—and I doubt not here also—toward the peoples of all the Russias and a resolve to persevere through many differences and rebuffs in establishing lasting friendships.

It is my duty, however, to place before you certain facts about the present position in Europe.

From Stettin in the Baltic to Trieste in the Adriatic an iron curtain has descended across the Continent. Behind that line lie all the capitals of the ancient states of Central and Eastern Europe. Warsaw, Berlin, Prague, Vienna, Budapest, Belgrade, Bucharest and Sofia; all these famous cities and the populations around them lie in what I must call the Soviet sphere, and all are subject, in one form or another, not only to Soviet influence but to a very high and in some cases increasing measure of control from Moscow.

The safety of the world, ladies and gentlemen, requires a unity in Europe, from which no nation should be permanently outcast. It is from the quarrels of the strong parent races in Europe that the world wars we have witnessed, or which occurred in former times, have sprung.

Twice the United States has had to send several millions of its young men across the Atlantic to fight the wars. But now we all can find any nation, wherever it may dwell, between dusk and dawn. Surely we should work with conscious purpose for a grant pacification of Europe within the structure of the United Nations and in accordance with our Charter.

In a great number of countries, far from the Russian frontiers and throughout the world, Communist fifth columns are established and work in complete unity and absolute obedience to the directions they receive from the Communist center. Except in the British Commonwealth and in the United States where Communism is in its infancy, the Communist parties or fifth columns constitute a growing challenge and peril to Christian civilization.

The outlook is also anxious in the Far East and especially in Manchuria. The agreement which was made at Yalta, to which I was a party, was extremely favorable to Soviet Russia, but it was made at a time when no one could say that the German war might not extend all through the summer and autumn of 1945 and when the Japanese war was expected by the best judges to last for a further eighteen months from the end of the German war.

I repulse the idea that a new war is inevitable—still more that it is imminent. It is because I am sure that our fortunes are still in our own hands and that we hold the power to save the future, that I feel the duty to speak out now that I have the occasion and the opportunity to do so.

I do not believe that Soviet Russia desires war. What they desire is the fruits of war and the indefinite expansion of their power and doctrines.

But what we have to consider here today while time remains, is the permanent prevention of war and the establishment of conditions of freedom and democracy a rapidly as possible in all countries. Our difficulties and dangers will not be removed by closing our eyes to them. They will not be removed by mere waiting to see what happens; nor will they be removed by a policy of appeasement.

What is needed is a settlement, and the longer this is delayed, the more difficult it will be and the greater our dangers will become.

From what I have seen of our Russian friends and allies during the war, I am convinced that there is nothing they admire so much as strength, and there is nothing for which they have less respect than for weakness, especially military weakness.

For that reason the old doctrine of a balance of power is unsound. We cannot afford, it we can help it, to work on narrow margins, offering temptations to a trial of strength.

Last time I saw it all coming and I cried aloud to my own fellow countrymen and to the world, but no one paid any attention. Up till the year 1933 or even 1935, Germany might have been saved from the awful fate which has overtaken her and we might all have been spared the miseries Hitler let loose upon mankind.

There never was a war in history easier to prevent by timely action than the one which has just desolated such great areas of the globe. It could have been prevented, in my belief, without the firing of a single shot, and Germany might be powerful, prosperous and honored today; but no one would listen and one by one we were all sucked into the awful whirlpool.

We must not let it happen again. This can only be achieved by reaching now, in 1946, a good understanding on all points with Russia under the general authority of the United Nations Organization and by the maintenance of that good understanding through many peaceful years, by the whole strength of the English-speaking world and all its connections.

If the population of the English-speaking Commonwealth be added to that of the United States, with all that such cooperation implies in the air, on the sea, all over the globe, and in science and in industry, and in moral force, there will be no quivering, precarious balance of power to offer its temptation to ambition or adventure. On the contrary there will be an overwhelming assurance of security.

If we adhere faithfully to the Charter of the United Nations and walk forward in sedate and sober strength, seeking no one's land or treasure, seeking to lay no arbitrary control upon the thoughts of men, if all British moral and material forces and convictions are joined with your own in fraternal association, the high roads of the future will be clear, not only for us but for all, not only for our time but for a century to come.

Winston Churchill, March 5, 1946

---

Available at http://www.fordham.edu/halsall/mod/churchill-iron.html.

## DISCUSSION QUESTIONS
1. How did Churchill's "Iron Curtain" follow, or deviate from, earlier divisions of Europe?

2. Does the "Iron Curtain" model represent a fundamental change in Great Power relations? In what ways?

# Brezhnev Doctrine (September 25, 1968)

*In August 1968, the Soviet Union led a Warsaw Pact invasion of Czechoslovakia, which was implementing a reform agenda under the Communist Party Secretary Alexander Dubček. The program, which included a relaxation of censorship and travel restrictions, was called "Socialism with a human face." However, the Soviet leadership deemed Dubček's reforms as "anti-socialist." In a speech to Polish workers, Soviet Premier Leonid Brezhnev explained and justified the invasion.*

In connection with the events in Czechoslovakia the question of the correlation and interdependence of the national interests of the socialist countries and their international duties acquire particular topical and acute importance. The measures taken by the Soviet Union, jointly with other socialist countries, in defending the socialist gains of the Czechoslovak people are of great significance for strengthening the socialist community, which is the main achievement of the international working class.

We cannot ignore the assertions, held in some places, that the actions of the five socialist countries run counter to the Marxist-Leninist principle of sovereignty and the rights of nations to self-determination.

The groundlessness of such reasoning consists primarily in that it is based on an abstract, nonclass approach to the question of sovereignty and the rights of nations to self-determination.

The peoples of the socialist countries and Communist parties certainly do have and should have freedom for determining the ways of advance of their respective countries.

However, none of their decisions should damage either socialism in their country or the fundamental interests of other socialist countries, and the whole working class movement, which is working for socialism.

This means that each Communist party is responsible not only to its own people, but also to all the socialist countries, to the entire Communist movement. Whoever forget this, in stressing only the independence of the Communist party, becomes one-sided. He deviates from his international duty.

Marxist dialectics are opposed to one-sidedness. They demand that each phenomenon be examined concretely, in general connection with other phenomena, with other processes.

Just as, in Lenin's words, a man living in a society cannot be free from the society, one or another socialist state, staying in a system of other states composing the socialist community, cannot be free from the common interests of that community.

The sovereignty of each socialist country cannot be opposed to the interests of the world of socialism, of the world revolutionary movement. Lenin demanded that all Communists fight against small-nation narrowmindedness, seclusion and isolation, consider the whole and the general, subordinate the particular to the general interest.

The socialist states respect the democratic norms of international law. They have proved this more than once in practice, by coming out resolutely against the attempts of imperialism to violate the sovereignty and independence of nations.

It is from these same positions that they reject the leftist, adventurist conception of "exporting revolution," of "bringing happiness" to other peoples.

However, from a Marxist point of view, the norms of law, including the norms of mutual relations of the socialist countries, cannot be interpreted narrowly, formally, and in isolation from the general context of class struggle in the modern world. The socialist countries resolutely come out against the exporting and importing of counterrevolution.

Each Communist party is free to apply the basic principles of Marxism[-]Leninism and of socialism in its country, but it cannot depart from these principles (assuming, naturally, that it remains a Communist party).

Concretely, this means, first of all, in its activity, each Communist party cannot but take into account such a decisive fact of our time as the struggle between two opposing social systems—capitalism and socialism.

This is an objective struggle, a fact not depending on the will of the people, and stipulated by the world's being split into two opposite social systems. Lenin said: "Each man must choose between joining our side or the other side. Any attempt to avoid taking sides in this issue must end in fiasco."

It has got to be emphasized that when a socialist country seems to adopt a "nonaffiliated" stand, it retains its national independence, in effect, precisely because of the might of the socialist community, and above all the Soviet Union as a central force, which also includes the might of its armed forces. The weakening of any of the links in the world system of socialism directly affects all the socialist countries, which cannot look indifferently upon this.

The antisocialist elements in Czechoslovakia actually covered up the demand for so-called neutrality and Czechoslovakia's withdrawal from the socialist community with talking about the right of nations to self-determination.

However, the implementation of such "self-determination," in other words, Czechoslovakia's detachment from the socialist community, would have come into conflict with its own vital interests and would have been detrimental to the other socialist states.

Such "self-determination," as a result of which NATO troops would have been able to come up to the Soviet border, while the community of European socialist countries would have been split, in effect encroaches upon the vital interests of the peoples of these countries and conflicts, as the very root of it, with the right of these people to socialist self-determination.

Discharging their internationalist duty toward the fraternal peoples of Czechoslovakia and defending their own socialist gains, the U.S.S.R. and the other socialist states had to act decisively and they did act against the antisocialist forces in Czechoslovakia.

*Pravda*, September 25, 1968; translated by Novosti, Soviet press agency. Reprinted in L. S. Stavrianos, *The Epic of Man* (Englewood Cliffs, NJ: Prentice Hall, 1971), 465–66.

## DISCUSSION QUESTIONS

1. What is the theoretical justification for the Brezhnev doctrine? What was the USSR claiming to accomplish?
2. Do the stated goals of the USSR in this document differ from the stated goals of the United States toward its allies?

## Changes in China

# Wei Jingsheng, The Fifth Modernization (December 1978)

*As Deng Xiaoping worked to consolidate power in the late 1970s, his primary rivals were the heirs of Mao Zedong, including the "Gang of Four" who, along with Mao, had orchestrated the Cultural Revolution of 1966–76. Deng's desire to introduce a market economy and deemphasize political ideology clashed with these views.*

*As part of his campaign, Deng called on the people to "seek truth from facts," encouraging criticism of the past regime that he could harness to help his cause. In Beijing, this policy manifested itself in the "Democracy Wall," a brick wall near Xidan Street in Beijing (now a popular shopping area), on which poems, slogans, and manifestos were posted, most of them anonymously, starting in December 1978.*

*Among the most prominent of these posters was Wei Jingsheng's "The Fifth Modernization." Zhou Enlai, China's former premier, had advocated four modernizations (to agriculture, industry, technology, and defense) to bring China forward. Wei, a twenty-eight-year-old electrician, who had been a Red Guard during the Cultural Revolution, criticized Deng Xiaoping as a dictator and argued that Democracy—the Fifth Modernization—was essential if China was to truly modernize.*

*Wei was rare in that he signed his poster, and his criticism of the government brought reprisals. He was arrested in March 1979, and sentenced to fifteen years in prison. He was released in 1993 but jailed again when his release failed to win Beijing the 2000 Olympic Games. Since his final release in 1997, he has lived abroad and continues to criticize the Chinese government's record on human rights and democracy.*

## I. Why Democracy?

People have discussed this question for centuries. And now those who voice their opinions at Democracy Wall have carried out a thorough analysis and shown just how much better democracy is than autocracy.

"People are the masters of history." Is this fact or merely empty talk? It is both fact and empty talk. It is fact that without the effort and participation of the people there can be no history. No "great helmsman" or "wise leader" could exist, let alone any history be created. From this we can see that the slogan should be "Without the new Chinese people, there would be no new China," not "Without Chairman Mao, there would be no new China." It's understandable that Vice Chairman Deng is grateful to Chairman Mao for saving his life, but why is he so ungrateful to all of those whose "outcries" propelled him back into power? Is it reasonable for him to say to them: "You must not criticize Chairman Mao, because he saved my life?" From this we can see that phrases like "people are the masters of history" are nothing but empty talk. Such words become hollow when people are unable to choose their own destiny by majority will, or when their achievements are credited to others, or when their rights are stripped away and woven into the crowns of others. What kind of "masters" are these? It would be more appropriate to call them docile slaves. Our history books tell us that the people are the masters and creators of everything, but in reality they are more like faithful servants standing at attention and waiting to be "led" by leaders who swell like yeasted bread dough.

The people should have democracy. When they call for democracy they are demanding nothing more than that which is inherently theirs. Whoever refuses to return democracy to them is a shameless thief more despicable than any capitalist who robs the workers of the wealth earned with their own sweat and blood.

Do the people have democracy now? No! Don't the people want to be the masters of their own destiny? Of course they do! That is precisely why the Communist Party defeated the Nationalists. But what became of all their promises once victory was achieved? Once they began championing a dictatorship of the proletariat instead of a people's democratic dictatorship, even the "democracy" still enjoyed by a tenth of a millionth of the population was displaced by the individual dictatorship of the "great leader." Even Peng Dehuai was denounced for following the orders of the "great leader" and airing complaints.

A new promise was made: If a leader is great, then blind faith in him will bring greater happiness to the people than democracy. Half forced, half willingly, people have continued to believe in this promise right up until the present. But are they any happier? No. They are more miserable and more backward. Why, then, are thing the ways they are? This is the first question the people must consider. What should be done now? This is the second. At present, there is absolutely no need to assess the achievements and failures of Mao Zedong. When Mao himself suggested this be done, it was only out of self-defense. Instead, the people should be asking themselves whether without the dictatorship of Mao Zedong China would have fallen into its current state. Are the Chinese people stupid? Are they lazy? Do they not want to live more prosperous lives? Or are they unruly by nature? Quite the opposite. How, then, did things get the way they are? The answer is obvious: The Chinese people should not have followed the path they did. Why, then, did they follow this path? Was it because a self-glorifying dictator led them down it? The truth is, even if people had refused to follow this path, they would still have been crushed by the dictatorship. And when no one could hear any other alternative, the people felt that this was the one and only path to take. Is this not deceit? Is there any merit in this at all?

What path was taken? It's often called the "socialist road." According to the definition formulated by our Marxist forefathers, the premise of socialism is that the masses, or what is called the proletariat, are the masters of everything. But let me ask the Chinese workers and peasants: Aside from the few coins you receive each month to feed yourselves with, what are you the masters of? And what do you master? It's pitiful to say it, but the truth is, you are mastered by others, even down to your own marriages!

Socialism guarantees that the producer will receive the surplus fruits of his labor after he has fulfilled his duty to society. But is there any limit to the amount of this duty? Are you getting anything more than the meager wage necessary to sustain your productive labor? Can socialism guarantee the right of every citizen to receive an education, to make full use of his abilities, and so forth? We can observe none of these things in our daily lives. We see only "the dictatorship of the proletariat" and "a variation of Russian autocracy"—that is, Chinese-style socialist autocracy. Is this the kind of socialist road the people need? Does dictatorship, therefore, amount to the people's happiness? Is this the socialist road Marx described and the people aspired to? Obviously not. Then what is it? As ridiculous as it may sound, it actually resembles the feudal socialism referred to in *The Communist Manifesto* as feudal monarchy under a socialist cloak. It's said that the Soviet Union has been elevated to socialist imperialism from socialist feudalism. Must the Chinese people follow the same path?

People have suggested that we settle all our old accounts by blaming them all on the fascist dictatorship of feudal socialism. I completely agree with this because there is no question of right or wrong. In passing, I would like to point out that the correct name for the notorious German fascism is "national socialism." It too had an autocratic tyrant; it too ordered people to tighten their belts; and it too deceived the people with the words: "You are a great people." Most importantly, it too stamped out even the most rudimentary forms of democracy, for it fully recognized that democracy was its most formidable and irrepressible enemy. On this basis, Stalin and Hitler shook hands and signed the German-Soviet Pact whereby a socialist state and a national-socialist state toasted the partition of Poland while the peoples of both countries suffered slavery and poverty. Must we go on suffering from this kind of slavery and poverty? If not, then democracy is our only choice. In other words, if we want to modernize our economy, sciences, military, and other areas, then we must first modernize our people and our society.

## II. The Fifth Modernization: What Kind of Democracy Do We Want?

\* \* \*

What is democracy? True democracy means placing all power in the hands of the working people. Are working people unable to manage state power? Yugoslavia has taken this route and proven to us that people have no need for dictators, whether big or small; they can take care of things much better themselves.

What is true democracy? It is when the people, acting on their own will, have the right to choose representatives to manage affairs on the people's behalf and in accordance with the will and interests of the people. This alone can be called democracy. Furthermore, the people must have the power to replace these representatives at any time in order to keep them from abusing their powers to oppress the people. Is this actually possible? The citizens of Europe and the United States enjoy precisely this kind of democracy and can run people like Nixon, de Gaulle, and Tanaka out of office when they wish and can even reinstate them if they so desire. No one can interfere with their democratic rights. In China, however, if a person even comments on the "great helmsman" or the "Great Man peerless in history," Mao Zedong, who is already dead, the mighty prison gates and all kinds of unimaginable misfortunes await them. If we compare the socialist system of "centralized democracy" with the "exploiting class democracy" of capitalism, the difference is as clear as night and day.

Will the country sink into chaos and anarchy if the people achieve democracy? On the contrary, have not the scandals exposed in the newspapers recently shown that it is precisely due to an absence of democracy that the dictators, large and small, have caused chaos and anarchy? The maintenance of democratic order is an internal problem that the people themselves must solve. It is not something that the privileged overlords need concern themselves with. Besides, they are not really concerned with democracy for the people, but use this as a pretext to deny the people of their democratic rights. Of course, internal problems cannot be solved overnight but must be constantly addressed as part of a long-term process. Mistakes and shortcomings will be inevitable, but these are for us to worry about. They are infinitely better than facing abusive overloads against whom we have no means of redress. Those who worry that democracy will lead to anarchy and chaos are just like those who, following the overthrow of the Qing dynasty, worried that without an emperor, the country would fall into chaos. Their recommendation was: Patiently suffer oppression! For without the weight of oppression, the roofs of your homes might fly off!

To such people, I would like to say, with all due respect: We want to be the masters of our own destiny. We need no gods or emperors and we don't believe in saviors of any kind. We want to be masters of our universe; we do not want to serve as mere tools of dictators with personal ambitions for carrying out modernization. We want to modernize the lives of the people. Democracy, freedom, and happiness for all are our sole objectives in carrying out modernization. Without this "Fifth Modernization," all other modernizations are nothing but a new promise.

Wei Jingsheng, *The Courage to Stand Alone: Letters from Prison and Other Writings*, edited and translated by Kristina M. Torgeson (New York: Penguin Books, 1998), 201–08.

## DISCUSSION QUESTIONS
1. Does Wei present himself as an opponent or a supporter of Deng Xiaoping's government?
2. Why does Wei state that democracy is essential for China's modernization?

# From: U.S. Embassy Beijing, To: Department of State, Wash DC, Student Demonstrations Update (December 24, 1986)

*This memo, reproduced from the National Security Archives, describes student protests in 1986. In December, university students in Shanghai and Beijing protested government involvement in campus life and called for the government to accelerate political reforms. The protests, which Jeffrey Wasserstrom has called "a virtual dress-rehearsal for Tiananmen," were put down peacefully.*

*Their most important effect in many ways was that they forced the resignation of Hu Yaobang—the general secretary of the Communist Party and a prominent advocate of reform in the government. Ellipses indicate deletions made by the State Department.*

## Confidential Beijing 32577

*E. O. 12356: DECL:OADR*
*Tags: PGOV, CH*
*Subject: Student Demonstrations Update*

*Ref: (A) Shanghai 8147 (B) Beijing 32085 (C) HK FBIS 230309Z Dec 86*

1. (C) Summary. A small student demonstration occurred in Beijing the evening of December 23. People's Daily published an editorial December 23 expressing sympathy with students aspirations but also making it clear that the limits of official toleration were being approached. PD December 24 ran a front page Q and A with the Shanghai Municipal Press spokesman which took a similar line. . . . In conversations with the ambassador December 23, expressed their views of the student situation. Wang took a relatively upbeat view, while the two Lius were more pessimistic. The demonstrations raise questions, as the PD editorial noted, about political stability, and there is no doubt that the authorities will crack down hard if political stability is threatened, particularly if student demonstrations continue or, worse, combine with labor unrest. If the demonstrations continue to phase down nationally as well as in Shanghai, they may do some, but not irreparable, damage to reform, particularly political reform; if demonstrations continue then many reform policies demonstrations grow significantly, become violent, or combine with labor, then many reform policies could be called into question and a major setback occur. To date, however, the official policy of avoiding the

use of force and even more importantly, on avoiding alienating the young people on whom China's future depends has resulted in remarkably sophisticated handling of the demonstrations which may serve to minimize damage. End summary.

2. (U) Although the student demonstrations continue to phase down, there is still some uncertainty as to the direction in which things will move. Students at Beijing universities were reportedly active for the first time the evening of December 23. About 1,000 students left Qinghua University at about 2100 moving toward other universities in the area. The crowd eventually grew to about 3,000 people. Police did not interfere and the demonstration dispersed after a while. A foreign journalist present at the demonstration was struck by the lack of seriousness of these demonstrators, although one demonstrator called loudly for "multi-party democracy." According to foreign journalists who observed the demonstration, the students did not leave the university area and did not reach Tiananmen Square.

3. (U) People's Daily December 23 published an editorial in a prominent position on its front page entitled "Treasure and Develop the Political Situation of Stability and Unity." The same editorial also appeared in Guangming Daily, the Beijing Daily and the overseas edition of the People's Daily. The editorial recalled both the successes of the past eight years of reform policy and the bitter experience of the cultural revolution. It observed that stability and unity are critical to the success or failure of modernization. It commented that the expression of differing views was permissible but that the adoption of "overly energetic methods" could influence stability and unity, and interfere with the normal functions of society. The editorial closed with a statement that "young people are our future and our hope" and they must be helped to understand the situation so that they too will work for peace and stability, and for the success of reform.

4. (C) A rebuttal of the PD December 23 appeared almost immediately on a bulletin board at Beijing University. The five-page "small character" poster was in letter format. Noting that the editorial was the first media reaction to the demonstrations in Shanghai, the writer refuted points in the editorial, asking

rhetorically just what "democratic channels" were available. The writer said that it ws [*sic*] clear from the editorial that there was no democracy. The writer made an unclear reference to an incident in which Japanese beat a Chinese, and disparaged the lack of action by Beijing University students. He raised themes of democracy, the legal system, political structural reform, and bureaucratism, recalled the September 28 demonstrations of last year, and claimed that 80 percent of Chinese are "numb." He suggested that students should go to work among villagers to gain an idea of the conditions there. About twenty students crowded closely around the poster at any given time, though with a constant turnover. There was little comment as they read, and those at the front were unwilling to read aloud for those in back.

5. (C) The December 24 People's Daily ran a Q and A on its front page filed by Xinhua Shanghai quoting the press spokesman of the Shanghai Municipal Government. The interview provided a good deal of descriptive matter about the Shanghai demonstrations and took the line that although it was understandable that students should be concerned about reform, the method that they had adopted, demonstrations, was incorrect. "A portion of the students," the spokesman said, "have insufficient understanding of the actual conditions of Chinese reform, and have a relatively unclear understanding about how democratic rights should be implemented."

6. (C) The authorities in Beijing continued to pull out all the stops to keep students in Beijing on campus. A large meeting for student activists was held at the Great Hall of the People December 23 where students were brought together with veterans of the fighting on the Vietnam border. City leaders also spoke to the students. Beijing radio stations carried lengthy accounts of this meeting with repeated references to the need for "stability and unity." The Beijing Daily December 24 carried an interview with 84-year-old Zhou Peifu, former president of Beijing University and vice chairman of the "September 3" Society (one of China's democratic parties), who said that he completely agreed with the PD editorial of December 23. He said that students did not realize that they were living in a

golden era, and that they should treasure stability and unity, and work for the modernization of China.

7. (C) At a December 23 luncheon hosted by . . . said that the student demonstrations were not all a bad thing, that young students needed a certain amount of outlet for their creativity. Of course, he added, serious disorder could not be condoned. But the spirit of the demonstrations was constructive. Wang recalled in this connection demonstrations he had seen in the United States in 1980 on an IV grant. There the demonstrations had been conducted in an orderly manner with rules of conduct observed by both sides. . . . [B]arely in the conversation that initial student demands related to "small things" such as tuition increases. Asked later on it students would be getting more freedom, he said that the extent to which their demands would be achieved remained to be seen. He also implied that the senior leadership was fully focusing on the demonstrations, and said that they had multiple sources of information, including both party and government channels.

\* \* \*

. . . , were pessimistic about the impact of the Student Demonstrations in a dinner discussion with the ambassador and Mrs. Lord on December 23. They were sympathetic with student aspirations for a more democratic society, but believed the protests would probably set back their cause. Opponents of political liberalization in the leadership would use the protests to underline the dangers of democracy, they believe. The students were understandably naive because of their inexperience and didn't realize the need to proceed with caution. The ambassador pressed . . . on their unqualified pessimism. He asked whether there might still be some beneficial impact if the demonstrations remained peaceful and amicable resolutions were reached. In that case, the prospects might be brighter, . . . but they remained skeptical. The process toward freer expression and participation, which they support, is clearly going to be a long and tricky one in their view. When the ambassador asked how else the students could convey their views to the authorities debating political reforms, . . . acknowledged that they could think of no other method.

9. (U) Political stability has always been a critical consideration in China. There can be no doubt that the authorities will crack down, and crack down hard, if stability seems to be being called into question. The Xinhua dispatch of December 21 made this clear implicitly and the People's Daily editorial of December 23 was even more explicit. On the other hand, the authorities have consistently taken the line that demonstrations are legal, and that students (or anyone else) have a right to express differing views. The critical issue for the authorities is certainly alienation—that is, how to avoid alienating young people who are, as PD said, "China's hope". Beijing mayor Chen Xitong expressed similar sentiments when he said at a December 22 cocktail party for foreign journalists that "students are not our enemy but our descendants." Beyond that there is the still more important question of moving from avoidance of alienation to achievement of the cooperation and support of young people in China's modernization and in the modernization of the party.

10. (U) There may be an additional complication. We have heard from journalists, and an article has appeared in the South China Morning Post (REF C) which refers to a strike over low wages which occurred at the Loyang, Henan Tractor Factory last week involving as many as 20,000 workers. The workers have apparently returned to work, and we have seen no reference to economic or labor-related issues in accounts of banners and posters carried by demonstrating students.

11. (C) Comment. We believe with Shanghai that a critical juncture has been reached. If the Shanghai demonstrations resume and grow, if large student demonstrations occur elsewhere, particularly Beijing, or if, worst of all, student and labor unrest combine, then the entire affair could become a net liability for reform with seriously negative policy consequences. A severe crackdown would be inevitable. If, on the other hand, the demonstrations phase down and out with the Shanghai demonstrations as the peak, it may be possible for the reform leadership to limit the damage done to reform, especially political reform. In any event, the question of the handling of the demonstra-

tions poses one of the most serious challenges the reform leadership has yet faced. End comment.

National Security Archive at George Washington University; available at http://www.gwu.edu/~nsarchiv.

## DISCUSSION QUESTIONS

1. What appears to have motivated these student protests?
2. Comparing this with the protests in 1989, what continuities do we see?

## East European Dissidents Speak Out

# Hungarian Revolution 1956: Sixteen Political, Economic, and Ideological Points, Budapest (October 22, 1956)

*In 1956, following Khrushchev's February speech condemning Stalin's crimes and cult of personality, reform movements emerged in several East European satellites, most notably Poland and Hungary. In October, Budapest university students issued the following statement, which was quickly supported by the Hungarian Writer's Union. The following day, fighting broke out in the capital and the Soviet Union led a Warsaw Pact invasion of Hungary. After weeks of fighting, the protests of students, intellectuals, and workers were put down and the communist reformer Imre Nagy was arrested and eventually executed. Future protest movements in the region looked to Hungary 1956 as both a warning and an inspiration.*

Students of Budapest!

The following resolution was born on 22 October 1956, at the dawn of a new period in Hungarian history, in the Hall of the Building Industry Technological University as a result of the spontaneous movement of several thousand of the Hungarian youth who love their Fatherland:

(1) We demand the immediate withdrawal of all Soviet troops in accordance with the provisions of the Peace Treaty.

(2) We demand the election of new leaders in the Hungarian Workers' Party on the low, medium and high levels by secret ballot from the ranks upwards. These leaders should convene the Party Congress within the shortest possible time and should elect a new central body of leaders.

(3) The Government should be reconstituted under the leadership of Comrade Imre Nagy; all criminal leaders of the Stalinist-Rákosi era should be relieved of their posts at once.

(4) We demand a public trial in the criminal case of Mihaly Farkas and his accomplices. Mátyás Rákosi, who is primarily responsible for all the crimes of the recent past and for the ruin of this country, should be brought home and brought before a People's Court of judgment.

(5) We demand general elections in this country, with universal suffrage, secret ballot and the participation of several Parties for the purpose of electing a new National Assembly. We demand that the workers should have the right to strike.

(6) We demand a re-examination and re-adjustment of Hungarian-Soviet and Hungarian-Yugoslav political, economic and intellectual relations on the basis of complete political and economic equality and of non-intervention in each other's internal affairs.

(7) We demand the re-organization of the entire economic life of Hungary, with the assistance of specialists. Our whole economic system based on planned economy should be re-examined with an eye to Hungarian conditions and to the vital interests of the Hungarian people.

(8) Our foreign trade agreements and the real figures in respect [to] reparations that can never be paid should be made public. We demand frank and sincere information concerning the country's uranium deposits, their exploitation and the Russian concession. We demand that Hungary should have the right to sell the uranium ore freely at world market prices in exchange for hard currency.

(9) We demand the complete revision of norms in industry and an urgent and radical adjustment of wages to meet the de-

mands of workers and intellectuals. We demand that minimum living wages for workers should be fixed.

(10) We demand that the delivery system should be placed on a new basis an[d] that produce should be used rationally. We demand equal treatment of peasants farming individually.

(11) We demand the re-examination of all political and economic trials by independent courts and the release and rehabilitation of innocent persons. We demand the immediate repatriation of prisoners-of-war and of civilians deported to the Soviet Union, including prisoners who have been condemned beyond the frontiers of Hungary.

(12) We demand complete freedom of opinion and expression, freedom of the Press and a free Radio, as well as a new daily newspaper of large circulation for the MEFESZ [League of Hungarian University and College Student Associations] organization. We demand that the existing 'screening material' should be made public and destroyed.

(13) We demand that the Stalin statue—the symbol of Stalinist tyranny and political oppression—should be removed as quickly as possible and that a memorial worthy of the freedom fighters and martyrs of 1848–49 should be erected on its site.

(14) In place of the existing coat of arms, which is foreign to the Hungarian people, we wish the re-introduction of the old Hungarian Kossuth arms. We demand for the Hungarian Army new uniforms worthy of our national traditions. We demand that 15 March should be a national holiday and a non-working day and that 6 October should be a day of national mourning and a school holiday.

(15) The youth of the Technological University of Budapest unanimously express their complete solidarity with the Polish and Warsaw workers and youth in connexion with the Polish national independence movement.

(16) The students of the Building Industry Technological University will organize local units of MEFESZ as quickly as possible, and have resolved to convene a Youth Parliament in Budapest for the 27th of this month (Saturday) at which the entire youth of this country will be represented by their delegates. The students of the Technological University and of the various

other Universities will gather in the Gorkij Fasor before the Writers' Union Headquarters tomorrow, the 23rd. of this month, at 2.30 P.m., whence they will proceed to the Pálffy Tér (Bern Ter) to the Bern statue, on which they will lay wreaths in sign of their sympathy with the Polish freedom movement. The workers of the factories are invited to join in this procession.

From *Report of the Special Committee on the Problem of Hungary, UN* General Assembly, Official Records: Eleventh Session, Supplement No. 18 (A/3592), p. 69. Available at http://www.fordham.edu/halsall/mod/1956hungary-16points.html.

## DISCUSSION QUESTIONS
1. How and why does Hungarian national identity play a role in the demands of the Hungarian students?
2. Why is Hungary's relationship to the Soviet Union a central concern of the Sixteen Points' authors?

# Helsinki Accords, Articles VII–IX (1975)

*In 1975, the United States, the Soviet Union and thirty-five European states signed the Conference on Security and Co-Operation in Europe Final Act. Designed to ease Cold War tensions, the act guaranteed the current borders of Europe, which was seen as a huge victory for the Soviet Union. However, Article VII: "Respect for human rights and fundamental freedoms, including the freedom of thought, conscience, religion or belief," provided a legal basis for the demands of liberal and intellectual dissidents in Eastern Europe.*

## VII. Respect for Human Rights and Fundamental Freedoms, Including the Freedom of Thought, Conscience, Religion or Belief

The participating States will respect human rights and fundamental freedoms, including the freedom of thought, conscience, religion or belief, for all without distinction as to race, sex, language or religion.

They will promote and encourage the effective exercise of civil, political, economic, social, cultural and other rights and freedoms all of which derive from the inherent dignity of the human person and are essential for his free and full development.

Within this framework the participating States will recognize and respect the freedom of the individual to profess and practice, alone or in community with others, religion or belief acting in accordance with the dictates of his own conscience.

The participating States on whose territory national minorities exist will respect the right of persons belonging to such minorities to equality before the law, will afford them the full opportunity for the actual enjoyment of human rights and fundamental freedoms and will, in this manner, protect their legitimate interests in this sphere.

The participating States recognize the universal significance of human rights and fundamental freedoms, respect for which is an essential factor for the peace, justice and well-being necessary to ensure the development of friendly relations and co-operation among themselves as among all States.

They will constantly respect these rights and freedoms in their mutual relations and will endeavour jointly and separately, including in co-operation with the United Nations, to promote universal and effective respect for them.

They confirm the right of the individual to know and act upon his rights and duties in this field.

In the field of human rights and fundamental freedoms, the participating States will act in conformity with the purposes and principles of the Charter of the United Nations and with the Universal Declaration of Human Rights. They will also fulfill their obligations as set forth in the international declarations and agreements in this field, including inter alia the International Covenants on Human Rights, by which they may be bound.

## VIII. Equal Rights and Self-Determination of Peoples

The participating States will respect the equal rights of peoples and their right to self-determination, acting at all times in conformity with the purposes and principles of the Charter of the United

Nations and with the relevant norms of international law, including those relating to territorial integrity of States.

By virtue of the principle of equal rights and self-determination of peoples, all peoples always have the right, in full freedom, to determine, when and as they wish, their internal and external political status, without external interference, and to pursue as they wish their political, economic, social and cultural development.

The participating States reaffirm the universal significance of respect for and effective exercise of equal rights and self-determination of peoples for the development of friendly relations among themselves as among all States; they also recall the importance of the elimination of any form of violation of this principle.

## IX. Co-operation Among States

The participating States will develop their co-operation with one another and with all States in all fields in accordance with the purposes and principles of the Charter of the United Nations. In developing their co-operation the participating States will place special emphasis on the fields as set forth within the framework of the Conference on Security and Co-operation in Europe, with each of them making its contribution in conditions of full equality.

They will endeavour, in developing their co-operation as equals, to promote mutual understanding and confidence, friendly and good-neighbourly relations among themselves, international peace, security and justice. They will equally endeavour, in developing their co-operation, to improve the well-being of peoples and contribute to the fulfilment of their aspirations through, inter alia, the benefits resulting from increased mutual knowledge and from progress and achievement in the economic, scientific, technological, social, cultural and humanitarian fields. They will take steps to promote conditions favourable to making these benefits available to all; they will take into account the interest of all in the narrowing of differences in the levels of economic development, and in particular the interest of developing countries throughout the world.

They confirm that governments, institutions, organizations and persons have a relevant and positive role to play in contributing toward the achievement of these aims of their co-operation.

They will strive, in increasing their co-operation as set forth above, to develop closer relations among themselves on an improved and more enduring basis for the benefit of peoples.

Available at http://www.hri.org/docs/Helsinki75.html#H4.7.

## DISCUSSION QUESTIONS
1. How did the Helsinki Accords seek to set limits on the Cold War structure of superpowers and satellite states?
2. Why was Article VII a catalyst for the development of dissident movements in Eastern Europe?

# Václav Havel, Power of the Powerless (1977)

*Inspired by the Helsinki Agreement, Czechoslovak intellectuals, many of whom had been involved in the 1968 Prague Spring reforms, created "Charter 77." This document, originally printed in a West German newspaper with 243 signatories, grew into a national movement of intellectuals, reform communists, and some Roman Catholic leaders. The Charter movement, led by playwright Václav Havel and other dissidents, petitioned the government against human rights violations. One of the founders of the charter was philosopher Jan Patočka, who died in 1977, shortly after being interrogated by the state police. Havel, who considered Patočka his mentor, dedicated his most famous essay "Power of the Powerless" to him. Some of Havel's most important contributions to the dissident movement throughout East and Central Europe were developed in this essay, which is excerpted here. Havel discusses "living in truth," which involved not conforming to the totalitarian regime, and contrasts dissidents with the metaphorical figure of the conforming "green grocer." Havel also comments on the importance of the Charter issued earlier that year.*

## III

The manager of a fruit-and-vegetable shop places in his window, among the onions and carrots, the slogan: "Workers of the world, unite!" Why does he do it? What is he trying to communicate to the world? Is he genuinely enthusiastic about the idea of unity among the workers of the world? Is his enthusiasm so great that he feels an irrepressible impulse to acquaint the public with his ideals? Has he really given more than a moment's thought to how such a unification might occur and what it would mean?

I think it can safely be assumed that the overwhelming majority of shopkeepers never think about the slogans they put in their windows, nor do they use them to express their real opinions. That poster was delivered to our greengrocer from the enterprise headquarters along with the onions and carrots. He put them all into the window simply because it has been done that way for years, because everyone does it, and because that is the way it has to be. If he were to refuse, there could be trouble. He could be reproached for not having the proper decoration in his window; someone might even accuse him of disloyalty. He does it because these things must be done if one is to get along in life. It is one of the thousands of details that guarantee him a relatively tranquil life "in harmony with society," as they say.

Obviously the greengrocer is indifferent to the semantic content of the slogan on exhibit; he does not put the slogan in his window from any personal desire to acquaint the public with the ideal it expresses. This, of course, does not mean that his action has no motive or significance at all, or that the slogan communicates nothing to anyone. The slogan is really a sign, and as such it contains a subliminal but very definite message. Verbally, it might be expressed this way: "I, the greengrocer XY, live here and I know what I must do. I behave in the manner expected of me. I can be depended upon and am beyond reproach. I am obedient and therefore I have the right to be left in peace." This message, of course, has an addressee: it is directed above, to the greengrocer's superior, and at the same time it is a shield that protects the greengrocer from potential informers. The slogan's real meaning, therefore, is rooted firmly in the greengrocer's existence. It reflects his vital interests. But what are those vital interests?

Let us take note: if the greengrocer had been instructed to display the slogan "I am afraid and therefore unquestioningly obedient," he would not be nearly as indifferent to its semantics, even though the statement would reflect the truth. The greengrocer would be embarrassed and ashamed to put such an unequivocal statement of his own degradation in the shop window, and quite naturally so, for he is a human being and thus has a sense of his own dignity. To overcome this complication, his expression of loyalty must take the form of a sign which, at least on its textual surface, indicates a level of disinterested conviction. It must allow the greengrocer to say, "What's wrong with the workers of the world uniting?" Thus the sign helps the greengrocer to conceal from himself the low foundations of his obedience, at the same time concealing the low foundations of power. It hides them behind the facade of something high. And that something is ideology.

Ideology is a specious way of relating to the world. It offers human beings the illusion of an identity, of dignity, and of morality while making it easier for them to part with them. As the repository of something suprapersonal and objective, it enables people to deceive their conscience and conceal their true position and their inglorious *modus vivendi,* both from the world and from themselves. It is a very pragmatic but, at the same time, an apparently dignified way of legitimizing what is above, below, and on either side. It is directed toward people and toward God. It is a veil behind which human beings can hide their own fallen existence, their trivialization, and their adaptation to the status quo. It is an excuse that everyone can use, from the greengrocer, who conceals his fear of losing his job behind an alleged interest in the unification of the workers of the world, to the highest functionary, whose interest in staying in power can be cloaked in phrases about service to the working class. The primary excusatory function of ideology, therefore, is to provide people, both as victims and pillars of the posttotalitarian system, with the illusion that the system is in harmony with the human order and the order of the universe.

The smaller a dictatorship and the less stratified by modernization the society under it, the more directly the will of the dictator can be exercised. In other words, the dictator can employ more or less naked discipline, avoiding the complex processes of relating to the world and of self-justification which ideology involves. But the more complex the mechanisms of power become, the larger and more stratified the society they embrace, and the longer they have operated historically, the more individuals must be connected to them from outside, and the greater the importance attached to the ideological excuse. It acts as a kind of bridge between the regime and the people, across which the regime approaches the people and the people approach the regime. This explains why ideology plays such an important role in the post-totalitarian system: that complex machinery of units, hierarchies, transmission belts, and indirect instruments of manipulation which ensure in countless ways the integrity of the regime, leaving nothing to chance, would be quite simply unthinkable without ideology acting as its all-embracing excuse and as the excuse for each of its parts.

* * *

## VII

Let us now imagine that one day something in our greengrocer snaps and he stops putting up the slogans merely to ingratiate himself. He stops voting in elections he knows are a farce. He begins to say what he really thinks at political meetings. And he even finds the strength in himself to express solidarity with those whom his conscience commands him to support. In this revolt the greengrocer steps out of living within the lie. He rejects the ritual and breaks the rules of the game. He discovers once more his suppressed identity and dignity. He gives his freedom a concrete significance. His revolt is an attempt to live within the truth.

The bill is not long in coming. He will be relieved of his post as manager of the shop and transferred to the warehouse. His pay will be reduced. His hopes for a holiday in Bulgaria will evaporate. His children's access to higher education will be threatened. His superiors will harass him and his fellow workers will wonder about him. Most of those who apply these sanctions, however, will not do so from any authentic inner conviction but simply under pressure from conditions, the same conditions that once pressured the greengrocer to display the official slogans. They will persecute the greengrocer either because it is expected of them, or to demonstrate their loyalty, or simply as part of the general panorama, to which belongs an awareness that this is how situations of this sort are dealt with, that this, in fact, is how things are always done, particularly if one is not to become suspect oneself. The executors, therefore, behave essentially like everyone else, to a greater or lesser degree: as components of the post-totalitarian system, as agents of its automatism, as petty instruments of the social auto-totality.

Thus the power structure, through the agency of those who carry out the sanctions, those anonymous components of the system, will spew the greengrocer from its mouth. The system, through its alienating presence in people, will punish him for his rebellion. It must do so because the logic of its automatism and self-defense dictate it. The greengrocer has not committed a simple, individual offense, isolated in its own uniqueness, but something incomparably more serious. By breaking the rules of the game, he has disrupted the game as such. He has exposed it as a mere game. He has shattered the world of appearances, the fundamental pillar of the system. He has upset the power structure by tearing apart what holds it together. He has demonstrated that living a lie is living a lie. He has broken through the exalted facade of the system and exposed the real, base foundations of power. He has said that the emperor is naked. And because the emperor is in fact naked, something extremely dangerous has happened: by his action, the greengrocer has addressed the world. He has enabled everyone to peer behind the curtain. He has shown everyone that it *is* possible to live within the truth. Living within the lie can constitute the system only if it is universal. The principle must embrace and permeate everything. There are no terms whatsoever on which it can co-exist with living within the truth, and therefore everyone who steps out of line denies it in principle and threatens it in its entirety.

Václav Havel, *Open Letters: Selected Writings, 1965–90,* selected and edited by Paul Wilson (New York: Knopf, 1991).

## DISCUSSION QUESTIONS

1. What does Havel mean by "living in truth"? How does it place responsibility on citizens as well as the government? How does the greengrocer come to live in truth?
2. What does Havel see as the role of ideology in the post-totalitarian system?

# Pope John Paul II, Homily For Mass
## (June 3, 1979)

*In October 1978, Archbishop of Krakow Karol Wojtyła was elected the first Slavic pope, John Paul II. Eight months after his inauguration he returned to his native Poland, where he toured the country and celebrated an outdoor Mass for thousands in Warsaw's Victory Square. His homily underscored the centrality of Christianity to Polish history and warned that Christ could not be forcefully kept out of any region of the world. He also acknowledged the hundreds of thousands of Poles who died in the Warsaw Ghetto, setting a precedent for public discussions of anti-Semitism in his native country. Listeners interpreted John Paul's homily as a call for religious freedom in communist Eastern Europe and throughout the world. The next ten years of his papacy were marked by his critique of communism, his support for the Solidarity movement, and his openness in discussing Jewish-Christian relations.*

To Poland the Church brought Christ, the key to understanding that great and fundamental reality that is man. For man cannot be fully understood without Christ, or rather, man is incapable of understanding himself fully without Christ.

Therefore Christ cannot be kept out of the history of man in any part of the globe, at any longitude or latitude of geography. The exclusion of Christ from the history of man is an act against man. Without Christ it is impossible to understand the history of Poland, especially the history of a people who have passed or are passing through this land. It is impossible without Christ to understand this nation with its past so full of splendor and also of terrible difficulties.

Today, here in Victory Square, in the capital of Poland, I am asking all of you, through the great eucharistic prayer, that Christ will not cease to be for us an open book of life for the future, for our Polish future.

I wished to kneel before this tomb to venerate every seed that falls into the earth and dies and thus bears fruit.

All that, the history of the motherland shaped for a thousand years by the succession of generations—among them the present generation and the coming generation—and by each son and daughter of the motherland, even if they are anonymous and unknown like the soldier before whose tomb we are now.

All that, including the history of the peoples that have lived with us and among us, such as those who died in their hundreds of thousands within the walls of the Warsaw ghetto.

All that, I embrace in thought and in my heart during this eucharist and I include it in this unique, most holy sacrifice of Christ, on Victory Square.

And I cry—I who am a son of the land of Poland and who am also Pope John Paul II—cry from all the depths of this millen[n]-ium, I cry on the vigil of the Pentecost:

Let your spirit descend
Let your spirit descend
And renew the face of the earth,
The face of this land.

*New York Times,* June 3, 1979, p. 12.

## DISCUSSION QUESTIONS

1. How was the pope's admonition that "Christ cannot be kept out of the history of man" an attack on the communist government of Poland?
2. What is the significance of the pope's reference to Poland's Jewish community?

# Lech Wałęsa, Nobel Peace Prize Speech (December 10, 1983)

*Lech Wałęsa was a leader of the independent trade union, Solidarity, which led strikes at the Gdansk Shipyard in 1980. In 1981, the Polish government under General Wojciech Jaruzelski declared martial law and arrested the Solidarity leadership. Martial law was lifted in 1983, but Wałęsa was not permitted to travel to Norway to receive the Nobel Prize for Peace. Bogdan Cywinski, an exiled Solidarity leader, delivered Wałęsa's lecture in his absence. In his speech Wałęsa emphasized his nonviolent approach to reform in Poland and his ties to the Polish pope John Paul II, a supporter of his movement.*

---

Your Majesty, Honourable Representatives of the Norwegian people,

You are aware of the reasons why I could not come to your Capital city and receive personally this distinguished prize. On that solemn day my place is among those with whom I have grown and to whom I belong—the workers of Gdansk.

Let my words convey to you the joy and the never extinguished hope of the millions of my brothers—the millions of working people in factories and offices, associated in the union whose very name expresses one of the noblest aspirations of humanity. Today all of them, like myself, feel greatly honoured by the prize.

With deep sorrow I think of those who paid with their lives for the loyalty to "Solidarity"; of those who are behind prison bars and who are victims of repressions. I think of all those with whom I have travelled the same road and with whom I shared the trials and tribulations of our time.

For the first time a Pole has been awarded a prize which Alfred Nobel founded for activities towards bringing the nations of the world closer together. The most ardent hopes of my compatriots are linked with this idea—in spite of the violence, cruelty and brutality which characterise the conflicts splitting the present-day world.

We desire peace—and that is why we have never resorted to physical force. We crave for justice—and that is why we are so persistent in the struggle for our rights, We seek freedom of convictions—and that is why we have never attempted to enslave man's conscience nor shall we ever attempt to do so.

We are fighting for the right of the working people to association and for the dignity of human labour. We respect the dignity and the rights of every man and every nation. The path to a brighter future of the world leads through honest reconciliation of the conflicting interests and not through hatred and bloodshed. To follow that path means to enhance the moral power of the all-embracing idea of human solidarity.

I feel happy and proud that over the past few years this idea has been so closely connected with the name of my homeland.

In 1905, when Poland did not appear on the map of Europe, Henryk Sienkiewicz said when receiving the Nobel prize for literature: "She was pronounced dead—yet here is a proof that She lives on; She was declared incapable to think and to work—and here is proof to the contrary; She was pronounced defeated—and here is proof that She is victorious".

Today nobody claims that Poland is dead. But the words have acquired a new meaning.

May I express to you—the illustrious representatives of the Norwegian people—my most profound gratitude for confirming the vitality and strength of our idea by awarding the Nobel Peace Prize to the chairman of "Solidarity".

---

Available at http://nobelprize.org.

## DISCUSSION QUESTIONS
1. Why does Wałęsa advocate a nonviolent approach to his country's crisis?
2. Wałęsa claims that he speaks "as a worker." How does this identity affect his views on Solidarity and the situation in Poland?
3. What role does religion play in Wałęsa's views?


# Adam Michnik, Letter from the Gdansk Prison (July 18, 1985)

---

*Adam Michnik was an intellectual leader of the Polish dissident movement. A member of KOR, the Workers' Defense Committee, Michnik was the editor of* samizdat *newspapers and journals. He was arrested and imprisoned several times during the 1980s for his participation in and support for Solidarity strikes. In this excerpt from his 1985 essay, written while imprisoned in Gdansk, Michnik discussed the tactics and achievements of Solidarity and Church opposition.*

---

It will soon be ten years since fifty-nine intellectuals signed a petition demanding that the scope of freedom in Poland be broadened. The petition also spoke of workers' rights to independent trade union. The letter of the fifty-nine became a warning. "You cannot govern like this any longer," was its message to Gierek. The authorities' only answer was to carry out reprisals against the people who signed it. A few months later Poland was shaken by another, incomparably more dramatic signal of crisis. In June 1976 workers in Random and Ursus went on strike, demonstrating in the streets against an enormous price increase. The reaction of the government was typical: the price increase was withdrawn and participants in the protests were forced to walk through gauntlets of truncheon-swinging police (so-called paths of health). They were tried, slandered, and made targets of hate propaganda. A spontaneous movement to help these workers emerged among the intelligentsia, giving birth to the Workers' Defense Committee (KOŘ) and the democratic opposition movement—the first links in the long chain of the new "miracle on the Vistula."

The ensuing events may be described as a dramatic wrestling match between the totalitarian power and the society searching for a way to attain autonomy. The period between August 1980 and December 1981 was merely a phase in this struggle. It ended with a setback for the independent society and a disaster for the totalitarian state. For disaster is an appropriate name for a situation where workers are confronted by tanks instead of debates. This is not the place for a detailed recounting of struggles that have taken place since then. Other people will take up this task; some, like Jan Józef Lipski in his book about KOR and Jerzy Holzer in *Solidarnosć*, have already made a beginning. I just want to stress two principal traits of the democratic opposition that were later adopted by Solidarity, namely the renunciation of violence and the politics of truth.

What were the sources of the power, the scope, the numbers, the patience and perseverance of this movement? Some explain them by pointing to a tradition of struggle for national independence, others detect the influence of the Catholic Church, still others praise the maturity of the Polish freedom strategy designed by the underground leaders. They are all right. But the principal reason can be found in the very essence of the totalitarian system which has long ago become a blocking factor in the development of creative forces, promoting sterility, destroying creativity and the spirit of society. The system exists only to protect the interests and the power of the ruling *nomenklatura* [i.e., high Party and state officials appointed by the top leadership or with its consent]. Since the Soviet Union regards the rule of the *nomenklatura* as a guarantee of its ideological and political stake in Poland, the Polish striving for autonomy threatens not only the power of the generals but also Soviet interests. Is it possible to change this particular definition of Soviet interests in Poland? The future of Polish independence depends on this question. The answer will also determine the nature of peaceful coexistence, because it will demonstrate whether Soviet leaders are willing to accept a new political reality.

Polish political reality is such that forty months after the imposition of martial law there exists a large opposition movement and an even more widespread front of refusal to cooperate with the generals. At the same time, Solidarity did not resort to terror, assassinations, or kidnappings. These methods belong exclusively to the repertory of the authorities. How can we explain this peculiar contradiction, which the official propagandists call "normalization"? What can we call this unusual situation where repression, provocations, and sheer exhaustion (the best ally of any dictatorship) have failed to annihilate Solidarity, the main organization of the civil-disobedience movement, or to push it into the blind alley of terrorism? How come our nation has been able to transcend the dilemma so typical of defeated societies, the hopeless choice between servility and despair?

It seems that the Polish nation does not think it has been defeated. The answer to the questions we posed can be found in Lenin's old adage, well known to the Communists: the regime cannot rule any longer according to the old ways, but it does not know how to change them; the people do not want to live according to the old ways, and they are no longer afraid to try new ones.

What does it mean that they "do not want to live according to the old ways?" It means that people don't want to be like objects, silently accepting their own enslavement; they reject their status as subjects, they wish to be masters of their own fate. And they are not afraid to do so.

But what does it mean "to rule according to the old ways"? It means to hope that the society is or will soon become completely terrorized and thus wholly molded by the state. Changing this sort of rule means to accept the autonomy of society not as a passing inconvenience but as an integral part of social reality. This is the road to dialogue and compromise.

Is this realistic? Is a compromise between the persecutor and his victim possible? Aren't our "fundamentalists" correct in maintaining that no democratic evolution is possible without a prior, total destruction of the Communist system and, therefore, the only sensible program of action must reject hopes for a future compromise with the ruling group and opt instead for the integral idea of independence, i.e., full independence from the Soviet Union and complete removal of Communists from power? This is the central dilemma of the Polish opposition movement.

*New York Review of Books*, 32, no. 12, July 18, 1985 (translated by Jerzy B. Warman).

## DISCUSSION QUESTIONS

1. What does Michnik claim are Solidarity's main contributions to the politics of opposition in Poland?
2. Why does Michnik believe that the nature of totalitarianism is the most important factor in understanding the success of Polish opposition?
3. What is the central dilemma of the Polish opposition movement?

## Cold War Leadership at the End of the Cold War

# Ronald Reagan, Tear Down This Wall Speech, Berlin (1987)

*In June 1987, Ronald Reagan gave this famous address at the Berlin Wall, contrasting the economic miracle of West Germany with the decline of the communist East. Calling on Mikhail Gorbachev to "tear down this wall," Reagan returned to the familiar metaphor of the Berlin Wall, the defining symbol of the Cold War. By the time Reagan gave this speech, he had developed a close rapport with Gorbachev, who resented the challenging tone of the remarks.*

---

Thank you very much.

Chancellor Kohl, Governing Mayor Diepgen, ladies and gentlemen: Twenty-four years ago, President John F. Kennedy visited Berlin, speaking to the people of this city and the world at the City Hall. Well, since then two other presidents have come, each in his turn, to Berlin. And today I, myself, make my second visit to your city.

We come to Berlin, we American presidents, because it's our duty to speak, in this place, of freedom. But I must confess, we're drawn here by other things as well: by the feeling of history in this city, more than 500 years older than our own nation; by the beauty of the Grunewald and the Tiergarten; most of all, by your courage and determination. Perhaps the composer Paul Lincke understood something about American presidents. You see, like so many presidents before me, I come here today because wherever I go, whatever I do: Ich hab noch einen Koffer in Berlin. [I still have a suitcase in Berlin.]

Our gathering today is being broadcast throughout Western Europe and North America. I understand that it is being seen and heard as well in the East. To those listening throughout Eastern Europe, a special word: Although I cannot be with you, I address my remarks to you just as surely as to those standing here before me. For I join you, as I join your fellow countrymen in the West, in this firm, this unalterable belief: Es gibt nur ein Berlin. [There is only one Berlin.]

Behind me stands a wall that encircles the free sectors of this city, part of a vast system of barriers that divides the entire continent of Europe. From the Baltic, south, those barriers cut across Germany in a gash of barbed wire, concrete, dog runs, and guard towers. Farther south, there may be no visible, no obvious wall. But there remain armed guards and checkpoints all the same—still a restriction on the right to travel, still an instrument to impose upon ordinary men and women the will of a totalitarian state. Yet it is here in Berlin where the wall emerges most clearly; here, cutting across your city, where the news photo and the television screen have imprinted this brutal division of a continent upon the mind of the world. Standing before the Brandenburg Gate, every man is a German, separated from his fellow men. Every man is a Berliner, forced to look upon a scar.

President von Weizsacker has said, "The German question is open as long as the Brandenburg Gate is closed." Today I say: As long as the gate is closed, as long as this scar of a wall is permitted to stand, it is not the German question alone that remains open, but the question of freedom for all mankind. Yet I do not come here to lament. For I find in Berlin a message of hope, even in the shadow of this wall, a message of triumph.

In this season of spring in 1945, the people of Berlin emerged from their air-raid shelters to find devastation. Thousands of miles away, the people of the United States reached out to help. And in 1947 Secretary of State—as you've been told—George Marshall announced the creation of what would become known as the Marshall Plan. Speaking precisely 40 years ago this month, he said: "Our policy is directed not against any country or doctrine, but against hunger, poverty, desperation, and chaos."

In the Reichstag a few moments ago, I saw a display commemorating this 40th anniversary of the Marshall Plan. I was struck by the sign on a burnt-out, gutted structure that was being rebuilt. I understand that Berliners of my own generation can remember seeing signs like it dotted throughout the western sectors of the city. The sign read simply: "The Marshall Plan is helping here to strengthen the free world." A strong, free world in the West, that dream became real. Japan rose from ruin to become an economic giant. Italy, France, Belgium—virtually every nation in Western Europe saw political and economic rebirth; the European Community was founded.

In West Germany and here in Berlin, there took place an economic miracle, the Wirtschaftswunder. Adenauer, Erhard, Reuter, and other leaders understood the practical importance of liberty— that just as truth can flourish only when the journalist is given freedom of speech, so prosperity can come about only when the farmer and businessman enjoy economic freedom. The German leaders reduced tariffs, expanded free trade, lowered taxes. From 1950 to 1960 alone, the standard of living in West Germany and Berlin doubled.

Where four decades ago there was rubble, today in West Berlin there is the greatest industrial output of any city in Germany—busy office blocks, fine homes and apartments, proud avenues, and the spreading lawns of parkland. Where a city's culture seemed to have been destroyed, today there are two great universities, orchestras and an opera, countless theaters, and museums. Where there was want, today there's abundance—food, clothing, automobiles—the wonderful goods of the Ku'damm. From devastation, from utter ruin, you Berliners have, in freedom, rebuilt a city that once again ranks as one of the greatest on earth. The Soviets may have had other plans. But my friends, there were a few things the Soviets didn't count on—Berliner Herz, Berliner Humor, ja, und Berliner Schnauze. [Berliner heart, Berliner humor, yes, and a Berliner Schnauze.]

In the 1950s, Khrushchev predicted: "We will bury you." But in the West today, we see a free world that has achieved a level of prosperity and well-being unprecedented in all human history. In the Communist world, we see failure, technological backwardness, declining standards of health, even want of the most basic kind— too little food. Even today, the Soviet Union still cannot feed itself. After these four decades, then, there stands before the entire world one great and inescapable conclusion: Freedom leads to prosperity. Freedom replaces the ancient hatreds among the nations with comity and peace. Freedom is the victor.

And now the Soviets themselves may, in a limited way, be coming to understand the importance of freedom. We hear much from Moscow about a new policy of reform and openness. Some political prisoners have been released. Certain foreign news broadcasts are no longer being jammed. Some economic enterprises have been permitted to operate with greater freedom from state control.

Are these the beginnings of profound changes in the Soviet state? Or are they token gestures, intended to raise false hopes in the West, or to strengthen the Soviet system without changing it? We welcome change and openness; for we believe that freedom and security go together, that the advance of human liberty can only strengthen the cause of world peace. There is one sign the Soviets can make that would be unmistakable, that would advance dramatically the cause of freedom and peace.

General Secretary Gorbachev, if you seek peace, if you seek prosperity for the Soviet Union and Eastern Europe, if you seek liberalization: Come here to this gate! Mr. Gorbachev, open this gate! Mr. Gorbachev, tear down this wall!

I understand the fear of war and the pain of division that afflict this continent—and I pledge to you my country's efforts to help overcome these burdens. To be sure, we in the West must resist Soviet expansion. So we must maintain defenses of unassailable strength. Yet we seek peace; so we must strive to reduce arms on both sides.

Beginning 10 years ago, the Soviets challenged the Western alliance with a grave new threat, hundreds of new and more deadly SS-20 nuclear missiles, capable of striking every capital in Europe. The Western alliance responded by committing itself to a counter-deployment unless the Soviets agreed to negotiate a better solution; namely, the elimination of such weapons on both sides. For many months, the Soviets refused to bargain in earnestness. As the alliance, in turn, prepared to go forward with its counter-deployment, there were difficult days—days of protests like those during my 1982 visit to this city—and the Soviets later walked away from the table.

But through it all, the alliance held firm. And I invite those who protested then—I invite those who protest today—to mark this fact: Because we remained strong, the Soviets came back to the table. And because we remained strong, today we have within reach the possibility, not merely of limiting the growth of arms, but of eliminating, for the first time, an entire class of nuclear weapons from the face of the earth.

As I speak, NATO ministers are meeting in Iceland to review the progress of our proposals for eliminating these weapons. At the talks in Geneva, we have also proposed deep cuts in strategic offensive weapons. And the Western allies have likewise made far-reaching proposals to reduce the danger of conventional war and to place a total ban on chemical weapons.

While we pursue these arms reductions, I pledge to you that we will maintain the capacity to deter Soviet aggression at any level at which it might occur. And in cooperation with many of our allies, the United States is pursuing the Strategic Defense Initiative—research to base deterrence not on the threat of offensive retaliation, but on defenses that truly defend; on systems, in short, that will not target populations, but shield them. By these means we seek to increase the safety of Europe and all the world. But we must remember a crucial fact: East and West do not mistrust each other because we are armed; we are armed because we mistrust each other. And our differences are not about weapons but about liberty. When President Kennedy spoke at the City Hall those 24 years ago, freedom was encircled, Berlin was under siege. And today, despite all the pressures upon this city, Berlin stands secure in its liberty. And freedom itself is transforming the globe.

In the Philippines, in South and Central America, democracy has been given a rebirth. Throughout the Pacific, free markets are working miracle after miracle of economic growth. In the industrialized nations, a technological revolution is taking place—a revolution marked by rapid, dramatic advances in computers and telecommunications.

In Europe, only one nation and those it controls refuse to join the community of freedom. Yet in this age of redoubled economic growth, of information and innovation, the Soviet Union faces a choice: It must make fundamental changes, or it will become obsolete.

Today thus represents a moment of hope. We in the West stand ready to cooperate with the East to promote true openness, to break down barriers that separate people, to create a safe, freer world. And surely there is no better place than Berlin, the meeting place of East and West, to make a start. Free people of Berlin: Today, as in the past, the United States stands for the strict observance and full implementation of all parts of the Four Power Agreement of 1971. Let us use this occasion, the 750th anniversary of this city, to usher in a new era, to seek a still fuller, richer life for the Berlin of the future. Together, let us maintain and develop the ties between the Federal Republic and the Western sectors of Berlin, which is permitted by the 1971 agreement.

And I invite Mr. Gorbachev: Let us work to bring the Eastern and Western parts of the city closer together, so that all the inhabitants of all Berlin can enjoy the benefits that come with life in one of the great cities of the world.

To open Berlin still further to all Europe, East and West, let us expand the vital air access to this city, finding ways of making commercial air service to Berlin more convenient, more comfortable, and more economical. We look to the day when West Berlin can become one of the chief aviation hubs in all central Europe.

With our French and British partners, the United States is prepared to help bring international meetings to Berlin. It would be only fitting for Berlin to serve as the site of United Nations meetings, or world conferences on human rights and arms control or other issues that call for international cooperation.

There is no better way to establish hope for the future than to enlighten young minds, and we would be honored to sponsor summer youth exchanges, cultural events, and other programs for young Berliners from the East. Our French and British friends, I'm certain, will do the same. And it's my hope that an authority can be found in East Berlin to sponsor visits from young people of the Western sectors.

One final proposal, one close to my heart: Sport represents a source of enjoyment and ennoblement, and you may have noted that the Republic of Korea—South Korea—has offered to permit certain events of the 1988 Olympics to take place in the North. International sports competitions of all kinds could take place in both parts of this city. And what better way to demonstrate to the world the openness of this city than to offer in some future year to hold the Olympic games here in Berlin, East and West? In these four decades, as I have said, you Berliners have built a great city. You've done so in spite of threats—the Soviet attempts to impose the East-mark, the blockade. Today the city thrives in spite of the challenges implicit in the very presence of this wall. What keeps you here? Certainly there's a great deal to be said for your fortitude, for your defiant courage. But I believe there's something deeper, something that involves Berlin's whole look and feel and way of life—not mere sentiment. No one could live long in Berlin without being completely disabused of illusions.

Something instead, that has seen the difficulties of life in Berlin but chose to accept them, that continues to build this good and proud city in contrast to a surrounding totalitarian presence that refuses to release human energies or aspirations. Something that speaks with a powerful voice of affirmation, that says yes to this city, yes to the future, yes to freedom. In a word, I would submit that what keeps you in Berlin is love—love both profound and abiding.

Perhaps this gets to the root of the matter, to the most fundamental distinction of all between East and West. The totalitarian world produces backwardness because it does such violence to the spirit, thwarting the human impulse to create, to enjoy, to worship. The totalitarian world finds even symbols of love and of worship an affront. Years ago, before the East Germans began rebuilding their churches, they erected a secular structure: the television tower at Alexander Platz. Virtually ever since, the authorities have been working to correct what they view as the tower's one major flaw, treating the glass sphere at the top with paints and chemicals of every kind. Yet even today when the sun strikes that sphere—that sphere that towers over all Berlin—the light makes the sign of the cross. There in Berlin, like the city itself, symbols of love, symbols of worship, cannot be suppressed.

As I looked out a moment ago from the Reichstag, that embodiment of German unity, I noticed words crudely spray-painted upon the wall, perhaps by a younger Berliner: "This wall will fall. Beliefs become reality." Yes, across Europe, this wall will fall. For it cannot withstand faith; it cannot withstand truth. The wall cannot withstand freedom.

And I would like, before I close, to say one word. I have read, and I have been questioned since I've been here about certain demonstrations against my coming. And I would like to say just one thing, and to those who demonstrate so. I wonder if they have ever asked themselves that if they should have the kind of government they apparently seek, no one would ever be able to do what they're doing again.

Thank you and God bless you all.

Ronald Reagan Foundation; available at http://www.reaganfoundation.org.

DISCUSSION QUESTIONS
1. How does Reagan use the Berlin Wall as a symbol of the Cold War?
2. Why does Reagan speak directly to Mikhail Gorbachev rather than to the leaders of East Germany when he asks for the Wall to be destroyed?

# Ronald Reagan, Farewell Address (January 1989)

*Reagan's final address as president of the United States, excerpted here, had a more conciliatory tone toward Gorbachev and the Soviet Union than his Berlin Wall speech. He gave credit to the Soviet leader for the reform movements of perestroika (rebuilding) and glasnost (openness) as well as his willingness to work with the West, extend freedoms, and release political prisoners.*

I won a nickname, "The Great Communicator." But I never thought it was my style or the words I used that made a difference: It was the content. I wasn't a great communicator, but I communicated great things, and they didn't spring full bloom from my brow, they came from the heart of a great nation—from our experience, our wisdom, and our belief in principles that have guided us for two centuries. They called it the Reagan revolution. Well, I'll accept that, but for me it always seemed more like the great rediscovery, a rediscovery of our values and our common sense.

Common sense told us that when you put a big tax on something, the people will produce less of it. So, we cut the people's tax rates, and the people produced more than ever before. The economy bloomed like a plant that had been cut back and could now grow quicker and stronger. Our economic program brought about the longest peacetime expansion in our history: real family income up, the poverty rate down, entrepreneurship booming, and an explosion in research and new technology. We're exporting more than ever because American industry became more competitive and at the same time, we summoned the national will to knock down protectionist walls abroad instead of erecting them at home. Common sense also told us that to preserve the peace, we'd have to become strong again after years of weakness and confusion. So, we rebuilt our defenses, and this New Year we toasted the new peacefulness around the globe. Not only have the superpowers actually begun to reduce their stockpiles of nuclear weapons—and hope for even more progress is bright—but the regional conflicts that rack the globe are also beginning to cease. The Persian Gulf is no longer a war zone. The Soviets are leaving Afghanistan. The Vietnamese are preparing to pull out of Cambodia, and an American-mediated accord will soon send 50,000 Cuban troops home from Angola.

The lesson of all this was, of course, that because we're a great nation, our challenges seem complex. It will always be this way. But as long as we remember our first principles and believe in ourselves, the future will always be ours. And something else we learned: Once you begin a great movement, there's no telling where it will end. We meant to change a nation, and instead, we changed a world.

Countries across the globe are turning to free markets and free speech and turning away from ideologies of the past. For them, the great rediscovery of the 1980s has been that, lo and behold, the moral way of government is the practical way of government: Democracy, the profoundly good, is also the profoundly productive.

When you've got to the point when you can celebrate the anniversaries of your 39th birthday, you can sit back sometimes, review your life, and see it flowing before you. For me there was a fork in the river, and it was right in the middle of my life. I never meant to go into politics. It wasn't my intention when I was young. But I was raised to believe you had to pay your way for the blessings bestowed on you. I was happy with my career in the entertainment world, but I ultimately went into politics because I wanted to protect something precious.

Ours was the first revolution in the history of mankind that truly reversed the course of government, and with three little words:

"We the people." "We the people" tell the government what to do, it doesn't tell us. "We the people" are the driver, the government is the car. And we decide where it should go, and by what route, and how fast. Almost all the world's constitutions are documents in which governments tell the people what their privileges are. Our Constitution is a document in which "We the people" tell the government what it is allowed to do. "We the people" are free. This belief has been the underlying basis for everything I've tried to do these past eight years.

But back in the 1960s, when I began, it seemed to me that we'd begun reversing the order of things—that through more and more rules and regulations and confiscatory taxes, the government was taking more of our money, more of our options, and more of our freedom. I went into politics in part to put up my hand and say, "Stop." I was a citizen politician, and it seemed the right thing for a citizen to do.

I think we have stopped a lot of what needed stopping. And I hope we have once again reminded people that man is not free unless government is limited. There's a clear cause and effect here that is as neat and predictable as a law of physics: As government expands, liberty contracts.

Nothing is less free than pure communism, and yet we have, the past few years, forged a satisfying new closeness with the Soviet Union. I've been asked if this isn't a gamble, and my answer is no because we're basing our actions not on words but deeds. The detente of the 1970s was based not on actions but promises. They'd promise to treat their own people and the people of the world better. But the gulag was still the gulag, and the state was still expansionist, and they still waged away proxy wars in Africa, Asia, and Latin America.

Well, this time, so far, it's different. President Gorbachev has brought about some internal democratic reforms and begun the withdrawal from Afghanistan. He has also freed prisoners whose names I've given him every time we've met.

But life has a way of reminding you of big things through small incidents. Once, during the heady days of the Moscow summit, Nancy and I decided to break off from the entourage one afternoon to visit the shops on Arbat Street—that's a little street just off Moscow's main shopping area. Even though our visit was a surprise, every Russian there immediately recognized us and called out our names and reached for our hands. We were just about swept away by the warmth. You could almost feel the possibilities in all that joy. But within seconds, a KGB detail pushed their way toward us and began pushing and shoving the people in the crowd. It was an interesting moment. It reminded me that while the man on the street in the Soviet Union yearns for peace, the government is Communist. And those who run it are Communists, and that means we and they view such issues as freedom and human rights very differently.

We must keep up our guard, but we must also continue to work together to lessen and eliminate tension and mistrust. My view is that President Gorbachev is different from previous Soviet leaders. I think he knows some of the things wrong with his society and is trying to fix them. We wish him well. And we'll continue to work to make sure that the Soviet Union that eventually emerges from this process is a less threatening one. What it all boils down to is this. I want the new closeness to continue. And it will, as long as we make it clear that we will continue to act in a certain way as long as they continue to act in a helpful manner. If and when they don't, at first pull your punches. If they persist, pull the plug. It's still trust but verify. It's still play, but cut the cards. It's still watch closely. And don't be afraid to see what you see.

Ronald Reagan Foundation; available at http://www.reaganfoundation.org.

## DISCUSSION QUESTIONS
1. Does Reagan's farewell address foreshadow the great events of 1989?
2. How does Reagan characterize his Soviet counterpart, Mikhail Gorbachev? Is this a revision of his remarks at the Berlin Wall two years earlier?

# Mikhail Gorbachev, Speech to the United Nations (December 7, 1988)

*Gorbachev's speech to the United States, excerpted here, announced a vast reduction of Soviet military presence in Eastern Europe and along the Chinese border, demonstrating his unwillingness to interfere in internal matters of the satellite states. Many historians credit this speech with giving dissidents the confidence to push harder for reform in their own countries.*

Two great revolutions, the French revolution of 1789 and the Russian revolution of 1917, have exerted a powerful influence on the actual nature of the historical process and radically changed the course of world events. Both of them, each in its own way, have given a gigantic impetus to man's progress. They are also the ones that have formed in many respects the way of thinking which is still prevailing in the public consciousness.

That is a very great spiritual wealth, but there emerges before us today a different world, for which it is necessary to seek different roads toward the future, to seek—relying, of course, on accumulated experience—but also seeing the radical differences between that which was yesterday and that which is taking place today.

The newness of the tasks, and at the same time their difficulty, are not limited to this. Today we have entered an era when progress will be based on the interests of all mankind. Consciousness of this requires that world policy, too, should be determined by the priority of the values of all mankind.

The history of the past centuries and millennia has been a history of almost ubiquitous wars, and sometimes desperate battles, leading to mutual destruction. They occurred in the clash of social and political interests and national hostility, be it from ideological or religious incompatibility. All that was the case, and even now many still claim that this past—which has not been overcome—is an immutable pattern. However, parallel with the process of wars, hostility, and alienation of peoples and countries, another process, just as objectively conditioned, was in motion and gaining force: The process of the emergence of a mutually connected and integral world.

Further world progress is now possible only through the search for a consensus of all mankind, in movement toward a new world order. We have arrived at a frontier at which controlled spontaneity leads to a dead end. The world community must learn to shape and direct the process in such a way as to preserve civilization, to make it safe for all and more pleasant for normal life. It is a question of cooperation that could be more accurately called "co-creation" and "co-development." The formula of development "at another's expense" is becoming outdated. In light of present realities, genuine progress by infringing upon the rights and liberties of man and peoples, or at the expense of nature, is impossible.

The very tackling of global problems requires a new "volume" and "quality" of cooperation by states and sociopolitical currents regardless of ideological and other differences.

Of course, radical and revolutionary changes are taking place and will continue to take place within individual countries and social structures. This has been and will continue to be the case, but our times are making corrections here, too. Internal transformational processes cannot achieve their national objectives merely by taking "course parallel" with others without using the achievements of the surrounding world and the possibilities of equitable cooperation. In these conditions, interference in those internal processes with the aim of altering them according to someone else's prescription would be all the more destructive for the emergence of a peaceful order. In the past, differences often served as a factor in pulling away from one another. Now they are being given the opportunity to be a factor in mutual enrichment and attraction. Behind differences in social structure, in the way of life, and in the preference for certain values, stand interests. There is no getting away from that, but neither is there any getting away from the need to find a balance of interests within an international framework, which has become a condition for survival and progress. As you ponder all this, you come to the conclusion that if we wish to take account of the lessons of the past and the realities of the present, if we must reckon with the objective logic of world development, it is necessary to seek—and the[n] seek jointly—an approach toward improving the international situation and building a new world. If that it so, then it is also worth agreeing on the fundamental and truly universal prerequisites and principles for such activities. It is evident, for example, that force and the threat of force can no longer be, and should not be instruments of foreign policy. * * *

The compelling necessity of the principle of freedom of choice is also clear to us. The failure to recognize this, to recognize it, is fraught with very dire consequences, consequences for world peace. Denying that right to the peoples, no matter what the pretext, no matter what the words are used to conceal it, means infringing upon even the unstable balance that is, has been possible to achieve.

Freedom of choice is a universal principle to which there should be no exceptions. We have not come to the conclusion of the immutability of this principle simply through good motives. We have been led to it through impartial analysis of the objective processes of our time. The increasing varieties of social development in different countries are becoming [a]n ever more perceptible feature of these processes. This relates to both the capitalist and socialist systems. The variety of sociopolitical structures which has grown over the last decades from national liberation movements also demonstrates this. This objective fact presupposes respect for other people's vie[w]s and stands, tolerance, a preparedness to see phenomena that are different as not necessarily bad or hostile, and an ability to learn to live side by side while remaining different and not agreeing with one another on every issue.

The de-ideologization of interstate relations has become a demand of the new stage. We are not giving up our convictions, philosophy, or traditions. Neither are we calling on anyone else to give up theirs. Yet we are not going to shut ourselves up within the range of our values. That would lead to spiritual impoverishment, for it would mean renouncing so powerful a source of development as sharing all the original things created independently by each nation. In the course of such sharing, each should prove the advantages of his own system, his own way of life and values, but not through words or propaganda alone, but through real deeds as well. That is, indeed, an honest struggle of ideology, but it must not be carried over into mutual relations between states. Otherwise we simply will not be able to solve a single world problem; arrange broad, mutually advantageous and equitable cooperation between peoples; manage rationally the achievements of the scientific and technical revolution; transform world economic relations; protect the environment; overcome underdevelopment; or put an end to hunger, disease, illiteracy, and other mass ills. Finally, in that case, we will not manage to eliminate the nuclear threat and militarism.

Such are our reflections on the natural order of things in the world on the threshold of the 21st century. We are, of course, far from claiming to have infallible truth, but having subjected the previous realities—realities that have arisen again—to strict analysis, we have come to the conclusion that it is by precisely such approaches that we must search jointly for a way to achieve the supremacy of the common human idea over the countless multiplicity of centrifugal forces, to preserve the vitality of a civilization that is possible that only one in the universe. * * *

Our country is undergoing a truly revolutionary upsurge. The process of restructuring is gaining pace; We started by elaborating the theoretical concepts of restructuring; we had to assess the nature and scope of the problems, to interpret the lessons of the past, and to express this in the form of political conclusions and programs. This was done. The theoretical work, the re-interpretation of what had happened, the final elaboration, enrichment, and correction of political stances have not ended. They continue. However, it was fundamentally important to start from an overall concept, which is already now being confirmed by the experience of past years, which has turned out to be generally correct and to which there is no alternative.

In order to involve society in implementing the plans for restructuring it had to be made more truly democratic. Under the badge of democratization, restructuring has now encompassed politics, the economy, spiritual life, and ideology. We have unfolded a radical economic reform, we have accumulated experience, and from the new year we are transferring the entire national economy to new forms and work methods. Moreover, this means a profound reorganization of production relations and the realization of the immense potential of socialist property.

In moving toward such bold revolutionary transformations, we understood that there would be errors, that there would be resistance, that the novelty would bring new problems. We foresaw the possibility of breaking in individual sections. However, the profound democratic reform of the entire system of power and government is the guarantee that the overall process of restructuring will move steadily forward and gather strength.

We completed the first stage of the process of political reform with the recent decisions by the U.S.S.R. Supreme Soviet on amendments to the Constitution and the adoption of the Law on Elections. Without stopping, we embarked upon the second stage of this. At which the most important task will be working on the interaction between the central government and the republics, settling relations between nationalities on the principles of Leninist internationalism bequeathed to us by the great revolution and, at the same time, reorganizing the power of the Soviets locally. We are faced with immense work. At the same time we must resolve major problems.

We are more than fully confident. We have both the theory, the policy and the vanguard force of restructuring a party which is also restructuring itself in accordance with the new tasks and the radical changes throughout society. And the most important thing: all peoples and all generations of citizens in our great country are in favor of restructuring.

We have gone substantially and deeply into the business of constructing a socialist state based on the rule of law. A whole series of new laws has been proposed or is at a completion stage. Many of them come into force as early as 1989, and we trust that they will correspond to the highest standards from the point of view of ensuring the rights of the individual. Soviet democracy is to acquire a firm, normative base. This means such acts as the Law on Freedom of Conscience, on glasnost, on public associations and organizations, and on much else. There are now no people in places of imprisonment in the country who have been sentenced for their political or religious convictions. It is proposed to include in the drafts of the new laws additional guarantees ruling out any form or persecution on these bases. Of course, this does not apply to those who have committed real criminal or state offenses: espionage, sabotage, terrorism, and so on, whatever political or philosophical views they may hold.

The draft amendments to the criminal code are ready and waiting their turn. In particular, those articles relating to the use of the supreme measure of punishment are being reviewed. The problem of exit and entry is also being resolved in a humane spirit, including the case of leaving the country in order to be reunited with relatives. As you know, one of the reasons for refusal of visas is citizens' possession of secrets. Strictly substantiated terms for the length of time for possessing secrets are being introduced in advance. On starting work at a relevant institution or enterprise, everyone will be made aware of this regulation. Disputes that arise can be appealed under the law. Thus the problem of the so-called "refuseniks" is being removed.

We intend to expand the Soviet Union's participation in the monitoring mechanism on human rights in the United Nations and within the framework of the pan-European process. We consider that the jurisdiction of the International Court in The Hague with respect to interpreting and applying agreements in the field of human rights should be obligatory for all states.

Within the Helsinki process, we are also examining an end to jamming of all the foreign radio broadcasts to the Soviet Union. On the whole, our credo is as follows: Political problems should be solved only by political means, and human problems only in a humane way. * * *

Now about the most important topic, without which no problem of the coming century can be resolved: disarmament. * * *

Today I can inform you of the following: The Soviet Union has made a decision on reducing its armed forces. In the next two years, their numerical strength will be reduced by 500,000 persons, and the volume of conventional arms will also be cut considerably. These reductions will be made on a unilateral basis, unconnected with negotiations on the mandate for the Vienna meeting. By agreement with our allies in the Warsaw Pact, we have made the decision to withdraw six tank divisions from the GDR, Czechoslovakia, and Hungary, and to disband them by 1991. Assault landing formations and units, and a number of others, including assault river-crossing forces, with their armaments and combat equipment, will also be withdrawn from the groups of Soviet forces situated in those countries. The Soviet forces situated in those countries will be cut by 50,000 persons, and their arms by 5,000 tanks. All remaining Soviet divisions on the territory of our allies will be reorganized. They will be given a different structure from today's which will become unambiguously defensive, after the removal of a large number of their tanks. * * *

By this act, just as by all our actions aimed at the demilitarization of international relations, we would also like to draw the attention of the world community to another topical problem, the problem of changing over from an economy of armament to an economy of disarmament. Is the conversion of military production realistic? I have already had occasion to speak about this. We believe that it is, indeed, realistic. For its part, the Soviet Union is ready to do the following. Within the framework of the economic reform we are ready to draw up and submit our internal plan for conversion, to prepare in the course of 1989, as an experiment, the plans for the conversion of two or three defense enterprises, to publish our experience of job relocation of specialists from the military industry, and also of using its equipment, buildings, and works in civilian industry. It is desirable that all states, primarily the major military powers, submit their national plans on this issue to the United Nations.

It would be useful to form a group of scientists, entrusting it with a comprehensive analysis of problems of conversion as a whole and as applied to individual countries and regions, to be reported to the U.N. secretary-general, and later to examine this matter at a General Assembly session.

Finally, being on U.S. soil, but also for other, understandable reasons, I cannot but turn to the subject of our relations with this great country. * * * Relations between the Soviet Union and the United States of America span 5 1/2 decades. The world has changed, and so have the nature, role, and place of these relations in world politics. For too long they were built under the banner of confrontation, and sometimes of hostility, either open or concealed. But in the last few years, throughout the world people were able to heave a sigh of relief, thanks to the changes for the better in the substance and atmosphere of the relations between Moscow and Washington.

No one intends to underestimate the serious nature of the disagreements, and the difficulties of the problems which have not been settled. However, we have already graduated from the primary school of instruction in mutual understanding and in searching for solutions in our and in the common interests. The U.S.S.R. and the United States created the biggest nuclear missile arsenals, but after objectively recognizing their responsibility, they were able to be the first to conclude an agreement on the reduction and physical destruction of a proportion of these weapons, which threatened both themselves and everyone else.

Both sides possess the biggest and the most redefined military secrets. But it is they who have laid the basis for and are developing a system of mutual verification with regard to both the destruction and the limiting and banning of armaments production. It is they who are amassing experience for future bilateral and multilateral agreements. We value this.

We acknowledge and value the contribution of President Ronald Reagan and the members of his administration, above all Mr. George Shultz. All this is capital that has been invested in a joint undertaking of historic importance. It must not be wasted or left out of circulation. The future U.S. administration headed by newly elected President George Bush will find in us a partner, ready—without long pauses and backward movements—to continue the dialogue in a spirit of realism, openness, and goodwill, and with a striving for concrete results, over an agenda encompassing the key issues of Soviet-U.S. relations and international politics.

We are talking first and foremost about consistent progress toward concluding a treaty on a 50 percent reduction in strategic offensive weapons, while retaining the ABM Treaty; about elaborating a convention on the elimination of chemical weapons—here, it seems to us, we have the preconditions for making 1989 the decisive year; and about talks on reducing conventional weapons and armed forces in Europe. We are also talking about economic, ecological and humanitarian problems in the widest possible sense. * * *

We are not inclined to oversimplify the situation in the world. Yes, the tendency toward disarmament has received a strong impetus, and this process is gaining its own momentum, but it has not become irreversible. Yes, the striving to give up confrontation in favor of dialogue and cooperation has made itself strongly felt, but it has by no means secured its position forever in the practice of international relations. Yes, the movement toward a nuclear-free and nonviolent world is capable of fundamentally transforming the political and spiritual face of the planet, but only the very first steps have been taken. Moreover, in certain influential circles, they have been greeted with mistrust, and they are meeting resistance.

The inheritance of inertia of the past are continuing to operate. Profound contradictions and the roots of many conflicts have not disappeared. The fundamental fact remains that the formation of the peaceful period will take place in conditions of the existence and rivalry of various socioeconomic and political systems. However, the meaning of our international efforts, and one of the key tenets of the new thinking, is precisely to impart to this rivalry the quality of sensible competition in conditions of respect for freedom of choice and a balance of interests. In this case it will even become useful and productive from the viewpoint of general world development; otherwise; if the main component remains the arms race, as it has been till now, rivalry will be fatal. Indeed, an ever greater number of people throughout the world, from the man in the street to leaders, are beginning to understand this.

Esteemed Mr. Chairman, esteemed delegates: I finish my first speech at the United Nations with the same feeling with which I began it: a feeling of responsibility to my own people and to the world community. We have met at the end of a year that has been so significant for the United Nations, and on the threshold of a year from which all of us expect so much. One would like to believe that our joint efforts to put an end to the era of wars, confrontation and regional conflicts, aggression against nature, the terror of hunger and poverty, as well as political terrorism, will be comparable with our hopes. This is our common goal, and it is only by acting together that we may attain it. Thank you.

Available at http://isc.temple.edu/hist249/course/documents/gorbachev_speech_to_UN.

## DISCUSSION QUESTIONS

1. What does Gorbachev mean when he calls for a "new world order" and a "consensus of all mankind"?
2. What did Gorbachev's foreign policy announcements encourage in political dissidents in the East-Central European satellite states?

# Part III
# 1989: The Year of Revolution

## The Soviet Union and East-Central Europe

## High Noon (1989)

*This poster was the most famous image created by Solidarity for the historic June 1989 elections. Solidarity used modern campaigning techniques never before seen in Poland, including catchy slogans and thought-provoking symbolism. The illustration depicts the American film actor Gary Cooper in his role as the sheriff in* High Noon, *the 1952 Western. Cooper wears the Solidarity emblem on his badge and carries a paper reading "elections." The caption reads "High Noon, June 4, 1989."*

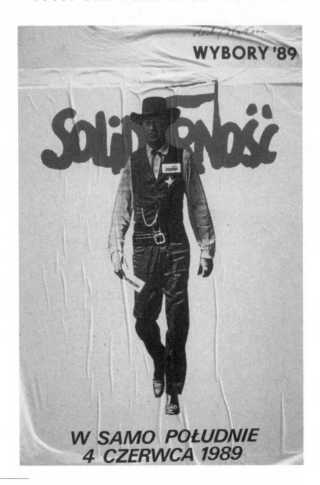

Chris Niedenthal/Time & Life Pictures/Getty Images.

DISCUSSION QUESTIONS

1. Why would Solidarity choose an image of an American actor for their election poster?

2. Why does the Solidarity artist consider June 4, 1989, a "High Noon" for Poland?

3. Does the poster have implications for the role of gender and masculinity in the Polish elections?

# Slobodan Milosevic, Speech at Kosovo Polje (June 28, 1989)

*The Communist Party of Yugoslavia experienced a slow decline rather than the rapid demise of other East European states. However, the seeds of future problems in the Balkans were sown in 1989. Serbian communist leader Slobodan Milosevic delivered the following speech to an estimated one million people at the central celebration marking the 600th anniversary of the Battle of Kosovo, held at Gazimestan on June 28, 1989. The battle had ended in the defeat of the Serb Kingdom by the Ottoman Empire, and in the late twentieth century, its memory and manipulation fueled Serb mistrust of Albanians, Slavic Muslims, and even Croatians in Yugoslavia, leading to the Yugoslav wars of the 1990s.*

By the force of social circumstances this great 600th anniversary of the Battle of Kosovo is taking place in a year in which Serbia, after many years, after many decades, has regained its state, national, and spiritual integrity.

Therefore, it is not difficult for us to answer today the old question: how are we going to face Milos [Milos Obilic, legendary hero of the Battle of Kosovo]. Through the play of history and life, it seems as if Serbia has, precisely in this year, in 1989, regained its state and its dignity and thus has celebrated an event of the distant past which has a great historical and symbolic significance for its future.

## Serbian Character—Liberational

Today, it is difficult to say what is the historical truth about the Battle of Kosovo and what is legend. Today this is no longer important. Oppressed by pain and filled with hope, the people used to remember and to forget, as, after all, all people in the world do, and it was ashamed of treachery and glorified heroism. Therefore it is difficult to say today whether the Battle of Kosovo was a defeat or a victory for the Serbian people, whether thanks to it we fell into slavery or we survived in this slavery. The answers to those questions will be constantly sought by science and the people. What has been certain through all the centuries until our time today is that disharmony struck Kosovo 600 years ago. If we lost the battle, then this was not only the result of social superiority and the armed advantage of the Ottoman Empire but also of the tragic disunity in the leadership of the Serbian state at that time. In that distant 1389, the Ottoman Empire was not only stronger than that of the Serbs but it was also more fortunate than the Serbian kingdom.

The lack of unity and betrayal in Kosovo will continue to follow the Serbian people like an evil fate through the whole of its history. Even in the last war, this lack of unity and betrayal led the Serbian people and Serbia into agony, the consequences of which in the historical and moral sense exceeded fascist aggression.

Even later, when a socialist Yugoslavia was set up, in this new state the Serbian leadership remained divided, prone to compromise to the detriment of its own people. The concessions that many Serbian leaders made at the expense of their people could not be accepted historically and ethically by any nation in the world, especially because the Serbs have never in the whole of their history conquered and exploited others. Their national and historical being has been liberational throughout the whole of history and through two world wars, as it is today. They liberated themselves and when they could they also helped others to liberate themselves. The fact that in this region they are a major nation is not a Serbian sin or shame; this is an advantage which they have not used against others, but I must say that here, in this big, legendary field of Kosovo, the Serbs have not used the advantage of being great for their own benefit either.

Thanks to their leaders and politicians and their vassal mentality they felt guilty before themselves and others. This situation lasted for decades, it lasted for years and here we are now at the field of Kosovo to say that this is no longer the case.

## Unity Will Make Prosperity Possible

Disunity among Serb officials made Serbia lag behind and their inferiority humiliated Serbia. Therefore, no place in Serbia is better suited for saying this than the field of Kosovo and no place in Serbia is better suited than the field of Kosovo for saying that unity in Serbia will bring prosperity to the Serbian people in Serbia and each one of its citizens, irrespective of his national or religious affiliation.

Serbia of today is united and equal to other republics and prepared to do everything to improve its financial and social position and that of all its citizens. If there is unity, cooperation, and seriousness, it will succeed in doing so. This is why the optimism that is now present in Serbia to a considerable extent regarding the future days is realistic, also because it is based on freedom, which makes it possible for all people to express their positive, creative and humane abilities aimed at furthering social and personal life.

Serbia has never had only Serbs living in it. Today, more than in the past, members of other peoples and nationalities also live in it. This is not a disadvantage for Serbia. I am truly convinced that it is its advantage. National composition of almost all countries in the world today, particularly developed ones, has also been changing in this direction. Citizens of different nationalities, religions, and races have been living together more and more frequently and more and more successfully.

Socialism in particular, being a progressive and just democratic society, should not allow people to be divided in the national and religious respect. The only difference one can and should allow in socialism are between hard working people and idlers and between honest people and dishonest people. Therefore, all people in Serbia who live from their own work, honestly, respecting other people and other nations, are in their own republic.

## Dramatic National Divisions

After all, our entire country should be set up on the basis of such principles. Yugoslavia is a multinational community and it can survive only under the conditions of full equality for all nations that live in it.

The crisis that hit Yugoslavia has brought about national divisions, but also social, cultural, religious and many other less important ones. Among all these divisions, nationalist ones have shown themselves to be the most dramatic. Resolving them will make it easier to remove other divisions and mitigate the consequences they have created.

For as long as multinational communities have existed, their weak point has always been the relations between different nations. The threat is that the question of one nation being endangered by the others can be posed one day—and this can then start a wave of suspicions, accusations, and intolerance, a wave that invariably grows and is difficult to stop. This threat has been hanging like a sword over our heads all the time. Internal and external enemies of multi-national communities are aware of this and therefore they organize their activity against multinational societies mostly by fomenting national conflicts. At this moment, we in Yugoslavia are behaving as if we have never had such an experience and as if in our recent and distant past we have never experienced the worst tragedy of national conflicts that a society can experience and still survive.

Equal and harmonious relations among Yugoslav peoples are a necessary condition for the existence of Yugoslavia and for it to find its way out of the crisis and, in particular, they are a necessary condition for its economic and social prosperity. In this respect Yugoslavia does not stand out from the social milieu of the contemporary, particularly the developed, world. This world is more and more marked by national tolerance, national cooperation, and even national equality. The modern economic and technological, as well as political and cultural development, has guided various peoples toward each other, has made them interdependent and increasingly has made them equal as well. Equal and united people can above all become a part of the civilization toward which mankind is moving. If we cannot be at the head of the column leading to such a civilization, there is certainly no need for us to be at its tail.

At the time when this famous historical battle was fought in Kosovo, the people were looking at the stars, expecting aid from them. Now, six centuries later, they are looking at the stars again, waiting to conquer them. On the first occasion, they could allow themselves to be disunited and to have hatred and treason because they lived in smaller, weakly interlinked worlds. Now, as people on this planet, they cannot conquer even their own planet if they are not united, let alone other planets, unless they live in mutual harmony and solidarity.

Therefore, words devoted to unity, solidarity, and cooperation among people have no greater significance anywhere on the soil of our motherland than they have here in the field of Kosovo, which is a symbol of disunity and treason.

In the memory of the Serbian people, this disunity was decisive in causing the loss of the battle and in bringing about the fate which Serbia suffered for a full six centuries.

Even if it were not so, from a historical point of view, it remains certain that the people regarded disunity as its greatest disaster. Therefore it is the obligation of the people to remove disunity, so that they may protect themselves from defeats, failures, and stagnation in the future.

## Unity Brings Back Dignity

This year, the Serbian people became aware of the necessity of their mutual harmony as the indispensable condition for their present life and further development.

I am convinced that this awareness of harmony and unity will make it possible for Serbia not only to function as a state but to function as a successful state. Therefore I think that it makes sense to say this here in Kosovo, where that disunity once upon a time tragically pushed back Serbia for centuries and endangered it, and where renewed unity may advance it and may return dignity to it. Such an awareness about mutual relations constitutes an elementary necessity for Yugoslavia, too, for its fate is in the joined hands of all its peoples. The Kosovo heroism has been inspiring our creativity for six centuries, and has been feeding our pride and does not allow us to forget that at one time we were an army great, brave, and proud, one of the few that remained undefeated when losing.

Six centuries later, now, we are being again engaged in battles and are facing battles. They are not armed battles, although such things cannot be excluded yet. However, regardless of what kind of battles they are, they cannot be won without resolve, bravery, and sacrifice, without the noble qualities that were present here in the field of Kosovo in the days past. Our chief battle now concerns implementing the economic, political, cultural, and general social prosperity, finding a quicker and more successful approach to a civilization in which people will live in the 21st century. For this battle, we certainly need heroism, of course of a somewhat different kind, but that courage without which nothing serious and great can be achieved remains unchanged and remains urgently necessary.

Six centuries ago, Serbia heroically defended itself in the field of Kosovo, but it also defended Europe. Serbia was at that time the bastion that defended the European culture, religion, and European society in general. Therefore today it appears not only unjust but even unhistorical and completely absurd to talk about Serbia's belonging to Europe. Serbia has been a part of Europe incessantly, now just as much as it was in the past, of course, in its own way, but in a way that in the historical sense never deprived it of dignity. In this spirit we now endeavor to build a society, rich and democratic, and thus to contribute to the prosperity of this beautiful country, this unjustly suffering country, but also to contribute to the efforts of all the progressive people of our age that they make for a better and happier world.

Let the memory of Kosovo heroism live forever!

Long live Serbia!

Long live Yugoslavia!

Long live peace and brotherhood among peoples!

---

Compiled by the National Technical Information Service of the U.S. Department of Commerce.

## DISCUSSION QUESTIONS

1. Although Milosevic discusses the benefits of Yugoslavia's multinational character, how does this speech represent a radical turn toward Serbian nationalism?
2. What does Milosevic see as the role of socialism in Yugoslavia?

# The "Great Coup" from the FRG
# Commentary (September 2, 1989)

*Throughout the summer of 1989, thousands of East Germans fled to the West through the newly opened border between Hungary and Austria. That fall thousands more took advantage of open borders to Czechoslovakia and Poland to floor the West German embassies in the neighboring states. East German propaganda insisted that the mass exodus of citizens was part of a well-planned coup attempt by West Germany. As East Germany prepared for celebrations of its fortieth anniversary as a state, the government propaganda agencies fought public opinion insisting on change.*

Planned long in advance and organized with care, a cloak-and-dagger operation was begun yesterday to take a larger number of GDR citizens from Hungary to West Germany in a move that was both illegal and in breach of international agreements, and surrounded by a large propaganda campaign.

This incident, unprecedented in international life and in the relations that exist between sovereign states, constitutes open interference in the internal affairs of the GDR and other countries. Those who are in charge in West Germany have made and financed this move in spite of all suggestions and warnings, contrary to all constructive proposals and initiatives on the part of the GDR that were designed to bring about a joint settlement of the issue. An unbridled malicious campaign of slander was launched against the GDR, overtly tempting away and deluding citizens of our state, misusing the opportunities for travel and contacts, with the help of the mass media and through direct actions.

Regrettably, representatives of the Hungarian People's Republic were induced to violate agreements and accords. International law and international agreements can by no means be cited to justify this decision, on the contrary they prohibit interference in internal affairs, disrespect for national laws and rules of other states as well as the arbitrary revocation or unilateral suspension of binding treaties and agreements.

The Bonn representatives are making full use of Hungary's position to promote their anti-socialist and revanchist goals. The socialist German state has supplied evidence of its patience and flexibility, but naturally it has also proved that it will not yield in questions of principle. It has made constructive offers vis-a-vis all states involved. It remains willing to keep open the road that leads back to law and order for those GDR citizens who wanted to leave our republic for whatever reason, to treat them with magnanimity. This is in line with the humanist nature of our social system. It is, however, only logical that attempts at political and economic blackmail, threats and enticements must be decisively rejected.

This coup from the FRG [Federal Republic of Germany] is neither an accidental nor a single move. It is part of imperialism's crusade against socialism as a whole in the course of which special prescriptions are given for each of the fraternal socialist states from Berlin through to Beijing.

Several things have seen a turn to the better in Europe, including relations between the two German states and between the GDR and West Berlin. The idea of a common European home is increasingly gaining ground.

Now one cannot but ask those in Bonn whether their alleged right to custodianship of all Germans may not be turning into a modern version of the notorious "back-to-the-Reich" movement, which treats human beings as mere objects of revanchism and chauvinism. The devastating consequences and innumerable human tragedies of such politics and practice should not be forgiven especially now as we are marking the 50th anniversary of the outbreak of the Second World War.

That the action is taking place at this particular point in time is not surprising. It was staged on the eve of the GDR's 40th anniversary. It is a situation in which the laws governing the class struggle inexorably come to the fore. Not everyone stands firm in the face of these challenges and pressures, and it happens that people leave their homeland due to the enemy's psychological warfare. The victory of socialism on German soil and 40 years of the socialist German state's successful development are an expression of the defeat of German imperialism. The enemies of socialism are trying to cover up historical turning points by staging provocations and propaganda campaigns, something they have done repeatedly in the course of history. With all attempts to put a spoke in the wheel of history having failed, imperialist circles now seem to believe that the chance of the century has come from them to take a kind of "social revenge" for the defeats they have suffered since the October Revolution of 1917.

The GDR as a cornerstone of peace and socialism at the divide between the two world systems through lures, promises and threats is subject to blackmail attempts aiming at forcing it into giving up fundamental principles and standards of value of socialism.

Official statements made in Bonn at the weekend have once more made it clear that organized human trafficking is being cloaked in the guise of humanitarianism. And once again it has been shown that August Bebel's words, "Be on your guard when your enemy commends you" have retained their validity.

The working people of the GDR through their performances and activities to mark the country's 40th anniversary are giving an appropriate response to these imperialist machinations. The powerful meeting in Berlins' Bebelplatz on the Day of Remembrance for the Victims of Nazi Terror and Day of Struggle Against Fascism and War as well as impressive actions in towns and villages throughout the GDR have unequivocally demonstrated people's commitment to their socialist state, to the policy of peace, disarmament and cooperation with all countries in the world. It is here, in this socialist state on German soil, that peace, humanism, material security and a sense of belonging have cast firm roots. It is here that everyone is needed and given every opportunity for self-realization. Socialism on German soil is an indispensable part of peace, security and stability in Europe. Our socialist system is just as irreversible as our alliance with the Soviet Union and our friendly relations with the other fraternal socialist states.

---

*Neues Deutschland*, September 2, 1989, found in German Propaganda Archive, Calvin College.

DISCUSSION QUESTIONS

1. How does East German propaganda characterize West Germany?
2. What evidence does the article give that East Germans still support their state?

# Günter Schabowski, Press Conference in the GDR International Press Center (November 9, 1989)

*As Party Secretary Erich Honecker celebrated the fortieth anniversary of the German Democratic Republic, his regime was crumbling beneath him. Protests broke out across East Germany, and Honecker was forced to resign in favor of Egon Krenz, an unpopular figure from the East German secret police who nonetheless promised reform. On November 9, Minister of Press and Information Günter Schabowski met with national and international journalists and announced that the Berlin Wall would open immediately. Berliners from both sides of the wall rushed to the center of their city, creating the most vivid images of 1989. The transcript of the press conference demonstrates the rapid changes taking place in a country and a government that had lost control.*

*Question.* My name is Ricardo Ehrman, representing the Italian press agency ANSA. Mr. Schabowski, you spoke about mistakes. Don't you believe that it was a big mistake to introduce this travel law several days ago?

*Schabowski.* No, I don't believe so. (Um) We know about this tendency in the population, this need of the population, to travel or to leave the GDR. And (um) we have ideas about what we have to bring about, (such as) all the things I mentioned before, or sought to mention in my response to the question from the TASS correspondent, namely a complex renewal of the society (um) and thereby achieve that many of these elements . . . (um) that people do not feel compelled to solve their personal problems in this way.

Those are quite a number of steps, as I said, and (um) we can't start them all at once. There are series of steps, and the chance, through expanding travel possibilities . . . the chance, through legalizing exit and making it easier to leave, to free the people from a (um) let us say psychological pressure . . . Many of these steps took place without adequate consideration. We know that through conversations, through the need to return to the GDR, (um) through conversations with people who find themselves in an unbelievably complicated situation in the FRG because the FRG is having a great deal of trouble providing shelter for these refugees.

So, the absorptive capacity of the FRG is essentially exhausted. There are already more than, or less than provisional (um), that these people have to count on, if they are put up there. (um). Shelter is the minimum for constructing an existence. Finding work is decisive, essential . . .

*Beil.* (softly) . . . integration . . .

*Schabowski.* . . . yes, and the necessary integration into the society, which cannot happen when one is living in a tent or an emergency shelter, or is hanging around unemployed.

So, we want . . . through a number of changes, including the travel law, to [create] the chance, the sovereign decision of the citizens to travel wherever they want. (um) We are naturally (um) concerned that the possibilities of this travel regulation—it is still not in effect, it's only a draft.

A decision was made today, as far as I know (looking toward Labs and Banaschak in hope of confirmation). A recommendation from the Politburo was taken up that we take a passage from the [draft of] travel regulation and put it into effect, that, (um)—as it is called, for better or worse—that regulates permanent exit, leaving the Republic. Since we find it (um) unacceptable that this movement is taking place (um) across the territory of an allied state, (um) which is not an easy burden for that country to bear. Therefore (um), we have decided today (um) to implement a regulation that allows every citizen of the German Democratic Republic (um) to (um) leave the GDR through any of the border crossings.

*Question.* (many voices) When does that go into effect? . . . Without a passport? Without a passport? (no, no)—When is that in effect? . . . (confusion, voices . . . ) At what point does the regulation take effect?

*Schabowski.* What?

*Question.* At once? When . . .

*Schabowski.* ( . . . scratches his head) You see, comrades, I was informed today (puts on his glasses as he speaks further), that such an announcement had been (um) distributed earlier today. You should actually have it already. So, (reading very quickly from the paper):

1) "Applications for travel abroad by private individuals can now be made without the previously existing requirements (of demonstrating a need to travel or proving familial relationships). The travel authorizations will be issued within a short time. Grounds for denial will only be applied in particular exceptional cases. The responsible departments of passport and registration control in the People's Police district offices in the GDR are instructed to issue visas for permanent exit without delays and without presentation of the existing requirements for permanent exit."

*Question.* With a passport?

*Schabowski.* (um . . . ) (reads:) "Permanent exit is possible via all GDR border crossings to the FRG. These changes replace the temporary practice of issuing [travel] authorizations through GDR consulates and permanent exit with a GDR personal identity card via third countries."

(Looks up) (um) I cannot answer the question about passports at this point. (Looks questioningly at Labs and Banaschak.) That is also a technical question. I don't know, the passports have to . . . so that everyone has a passport, they first have to be distributed. But we want to . . .

*Banaschak.* The substance of the announcement is decisive . . .

*Schabowski.* . . . is the . . .

*Question.* When does it come into effect?

*Schabowski.* (Looks through his papers . . . ) That comes into effect, according to my information, immediately, without delay (looking through his papers further).

*Labs.* (quietly) . . . without delay.

*Beil.* (quietly) That has to be decided by the Council of Ministers.

*Question.* ( . . . Many voices . . . ) You only said the FRG, is the regulation also valid for West Berlin?

*Schabowski.* (reading aloud quickly) "As the Press Office of the Ministry . . . the Council of Ministers decided that until the *Volkskammer* implements a corresponding law, this transition regulation will be in effect."

*Question.* Does this also apply for West Berlin? You only mentioned the FRG.

*Schabowski.* (shrugs his shoulders, frowns, looks at his papers) So . . . (pause), um hmmm (reads aloud): "Permanent exit can take place via all border crossings from the GDR to the FRG and West Berlin, respectively."

*Question.* Another question also: does that mean that effective immediately, GDR citizens—Christoph Janowski, Voice of America— does that mean that effective immediately, all GDR citizens cannot emigrate via Czechoslovakia or Poland?

*Schabowski.* No, that is not addressed at all. We hope instead that the movement will (um) regulate itself in this manner, as we are trying to.

*Question.* (many voices, incomprehensible question)

*Schabowski.* I haven't heard anything to the contrary.

*Question.* (many voices, incomprehensible)

*Schabowski.* I haven't heard anything to the contrary.

*Question.* (many voices, incomprehensible)

*Schabowski.* I haven't heard anything to the contrary. I'm expressing myself so carefully because I'm not up to date on this question, but just before I came over here I was given this information. (Several journalists hurry from the room.)

*Question.* Mr. Schabowski, what is going to happen to the Berlin Wall now?

*Schabowski.* It has been brought to my attention that it is 7:00 p.m. That has to be the last question. Thank you for your understanding.

(um . . . ) What will happen to the Berlin Wall? Information has already been provided in connection with travel activities. (um) The

issue of travel, (um) the ability to cross the Wall from our side, . . .
hasn't been answered yet and exclusively the question in the sense
. . . , so this, I'll put it this way, fortified state border of the GDR
. . . . (um) We have always said that there have to be several other
factors (um) taken into consideration. And they deal with the complex of questions that Comrade Krenz, in his talk in the—addressed
in view of the relations between the GDR and the FRG, in light of
the (um) necessity of continuing the process of assuring peace with
new initiatives.

And (um) surely the debate about these questions (um) will be
positively influenced if the FRG and NATO also agree to and implement disarmament measures in a similar manner to that of the
GDR and other socialist countries. Thank you very much.

Hans-Hermann Hertle, "The Fall of the Wall: The Unintended Self-Dissolution
of East Germany's Ruling Regime," *Cold War International History Project Bulletin*,
Fall/Winter 2001, 157–58.

## DISCUSSION QUESTIONS

1. How does the tone of the press conference reflect the government's loss of control in East Germany?
2. Why was unrestricted travel a particularly symbolic achievement for East Germans in 1989?

# Ferdinand Protzman, Clamor in the East: Jubilation in Berlin; a Day for Celebration and a Bit of Shopping (November 11, 1989)

*This article, published two days after the opening of the Berlin Wall, describes
the current euphoria in the once-divided city. It also highlights the disparities
between East and West Berlin, particularly in the availability of capital and
consumer goods.*

Church bells pealed, long-separated friends and family members
fell into each other's arms, people wept for joy and complete strang-

ers pressed money into newcomers' hands or offered them rides to wherever they wanted to go.

It was a day that made on indelible imprint on Berlin's collective memory. Hundreds of thousands of East Berliners crossed into West Berlin today, according to police estimates.

"The mood is just fantastic," said a woman from East Berlin. "The West Berliners have been wonderful to us. I thank them all." The East Berliners, coming from a land where nearly all prices are kept artificially low by subsidies, were also greeted by price-tag shock.

### 'But Cheap It's Not'

"It's all quite lovely," said a young woman from Rostock, as she gazed at the display window of a women's clothing store on the Kurfurstendamm, West Berlin's main street and the city's toniest shopping area. "But cheap it's not."

The sky was a high, clear blue and the "Berliner Luft"—the air of Berlin, that is lauded by natives for its invigorating qualities—overcame the usual pollution and lived up to its reputation. It rang with the sounds of celebration. The city center of West Berlin became a giant festival grounds, forcing police to ban auto traffic because of the press of pedestrians. Some restaurants gave out free food and drink. Bottles, cans and broken glass seemed to be everywhere.

### 'Now We Know the Way'

"The wall is gone!" Those slightly hyperbolic words were uttered countless times here in the last 24 hours, by people in both sides of the city. Although the forbidding concrete barrier still stands, it has fallen in the minds of East and West Berliners alike.

"I knew as soon as I heard the news on the radio last night what it meant," said Stani, a 19-year-old East Berliner, as he jostled for position in a West Berlin subway packed with East Germans on their way to celebrate on the Kurfurstendamm. "There is no turning back from this now. Allowing people to travel freely is a step that our Government can never retract. We won't be closed in again. The people will simply not allow that. Now we know the way here."

The celebration Stani and five of his schoolmates were going to join in grew throughout the day as more and more East Germans arrived in the West, many for the first time in their lives. What began late Thursday evening as a trickle of the curious, cautiously testing their Government's newly announced promise of free travel to the West, turned to a torrent today.

## Police Stop Counting

Police officials on both sides of the increasingly porous border simply stopped counting the East Germans who were crossing into West Berlin. Their best estimate was that hundreds of thousands had done so. West Berliners did not flock to the eastern half of the city, however, preferring, perhaps, to celebrate on their home turf.

Throughout the day, people poured through the border crossing points. As factories, schools and offices in East Berlin closed in the late afternoon, masses of people began moving in one direction— the border.

By 5 P.M. the Bornholmerstrasse border crossing point in the northeast section of the city was a sea of humanity. There were no formalities. Border guards on both sides merely waved the throng through and tried to direct traffic as best they could. A stream of East Berliners of all ages, walking seven abreast and stretching about 1,000 yards from end to end, filed across the border. They passed into West Berlin through a 60-yard-long gauntlet of cheering, whistling and applauding West Berliners. Autos and motorcycles were also lined up, and they honked their horns and flashed their lights as they crossed.

A 10-year-old boy, walking across with his parents and little brother, was nonplussed. Looking up at dozens of West Berliners shouting greetings as he stepped onto West German soil, he doffed his baseball cap, threw his arms in the air and cried, "Hello, fans." The crowd burst into laughter.

## Home from the Store

A few feet away, a counterflow of thousands of other East Berliners headed home, many carrying plastic bags from West Berlin supermarkets and department stores. Their purchases, often made possible by the 100 marks of "greeting money"—about $55—provided by the West German Government, range from groceries and cosmetics to used washing machines and satellite dishes.

There were block-long lines of East Germans at banks throughout West Berlin, where the money was given out. In an unprecedented step for a place with the most rigid business hours in Western Europe, West Berlin banks will be open on both Saturday and Sunday for East Germans wishing to pick up cash.

"We went in about midnight Thursday," said a 22-year-old East Berliner, sitting with her husband in their Soviet-built Lada as they waited in a line of cars to cross back into East Berlin at Bornholmerstrasse. On the backseat was a hand-painted Japanese fan, which they had purchased today.

The couple spent the night with the woman's grandmother in West Berlin, then drove around the city shopping and just looking. While they had been allowed to visit the city twice previously to see the woman's grandmother, they said today was different.

*New York Times*, November 11, 1989.

## DISCUSSION QUESTIONS
1. What is the mood in Berlin immediately after the fall of the Wall?
2. What clues does the article give that integration of West and East Germany will be a difficult process?

# Premier Ladislav Adamec, Speech at an Extraordinary Session of the CC CPCz, Prague (November 24, 1989)

*A week into the demonstrations in Prague, prime minister of Czechoslovakia Ladislav Adamec met with a special session of the Czechoslovak Communist Party Central Committee. A moderate, especially compared to the President Gustav Husák, Adamec called on his fellow communist leaders to find a politi-*

*cal solution to the upheavals in the capital. He recognized that a violent response from the government would only embolden and embitter the opposition; yet he maintained the goal of protecting socialism in Czechoslovakia.*

---

Making decisions is not simple. Events are developing rapidly and aren't the same everywhere. I therefore regard it as my duty to express my opinion of the situation and its resolution. I am aware we don't have much choice. The pressure of circumstances is rising day by day and possibly hour by hour. We have to deal with it. I am considering the alternatives along with everybody else. There are basically two ways to go—both have their advantages and drawbacks, merits and risks. None of them are guaranteed to fully succeed. With these thoughts, following on from what Comrade Jakeš has said, I would like to contribute to finding the internationally and internally optimum political variant. To explain the first alternative, let us assume that mass demonstrations and the spreading strike movements constitute a direct attack on the socialist establishment, and that therefore there is no other way but to immediately halt all protest actions. On the basis of this evaluation, we may decide that a general strike must be prevented even at the cost of extensive use of extraordinary means, including force. This operation could be complemented by a large number of protest letters from Party collectives in industrial and agricultural factories and other workplaces. One cannot passively watch the law being violated. To allow anarchy would be the direct opposite of democracy, whereas taking extraordinary measures could, if only temporarily, return calm to the streets. But experience with administrative measures has shown a significant risk. After a certain period the situation could explode again, bringing in another crisis, with still more unpredictable results.

For all these reasons, I would clearly prefer the second alternative: a political solution. We must count on making certain acceptable concessions. I believe that we have not nearly exhausted these possibilities. I also rely on the fact that most of our people, including young people, have no reason to be against socialism. They are unsatisfied with many things, even stirred up by all kinds of disinformation, but are able and willing to repay trust with trust. To drive the young generation into the arms of the enemies of social-ism would be an unforgivable mistake. This must be prevented under any circumstances. I also advocate political methods because the recent intervention of the forces of order has led to the radical-ization of youth, allowed the unification of various groups behind its condemnation, and has not contributed to the authority of ei-ther the Party or the state. Next time we have to avoid things like this. It would also be a mistake to underestimate the international risks of a broad application of force. We mustn't labor under the illusion that various democratization, environmental, and other movements end at our borders. Also, signed international treaties dealing with human rights cannot be taken lightly. When selecting methods of managing internal political problems, the international support of the socialist countries can no longer be counted on. From the capitalist states, one must take into account the results of a political and economic boycott. This warning should not be un-derstood as a call for concessions at any price, without regard to the loss of socialist values.

To look truth in the eye means to realize that the loss of political trust as a result of mistakes in leadership must be paid for. And there have been many in the last twenty years, and not small ones. I am convinced, however, that we need not pay too high a price, if we can manage to mobilize the Party. No one else has such a nu-merous membership, such an experienced cadre of functionaries, and close connections with each collective. * * * Today it has come down to the very status of the Party in society. If our meeting helps to energize all its members, it will fulfil its historic mission. If not, we shall pay dearly, and only very slowly repair the damage. I con-sider it especially important and sensitive to take a position on the basic demands, especially those most often voiced. They are ex-tremely varied, correct and incorrect, feasible either now or only later. This must be clear. Those that we are unable to answer im-mediately, at least let us say when we will address them. Under no circumstances should there arise the impression that we are avoid-ing something, using delaying tactics, and somehow maneuvering. Let us choose our course so as not to give impetus to further waves of still-more-radical demands. I consider it crucial to announce the calling of another meeting of the Central Committee within a fortnight to evaluate political questions, especially the program of accelerated restructuring and expanded dialogue. We would gain time, mobilize the Party, and improve its level of information on the chosen strategy. The Party needs a short-term action program, a plan for the unification of the greatest possible number of Communists towards a concrete goal in the upcoming weeks. It would then even be possible to organize a broad public discussion centered on the positions and proposal of the CC CPCz. We could also, for example, quickly submit proposals on the constitution for public discussion, publicize proposed laws on the association and assembly for citizen comment. This would provide a certain framework and solid content to a thus far less than constructive exchange of views. We could take the wind out of the sails of the daily proclamations, various calls, and petitions. I am convinced that only an active approach can put our side on the initiative, and with this we shall also gain the majority of our citizens in favor of Party policy. This is the best reply to the demands of Party organizations for more assistance from the CPCz Central Committee.

---

Stenographic minutes of the Extraordinary Session of the CC CPCz, November 24, 1989, pp. 21–23, State Central Archive, Prague, CC CPCz record group, W-0154/89.

## DISCUSSION QUESTIONS
1. What does Adamec mean by proposing a "political solution" to the situation in Czechoslovakia?
2. Does Adamec seem to recognize that communism is about to fall in his country?

# Transcript of the Closed Trial of Nicolae and Elena Ceaușescu (December 25, 1989)

---

*The most repressive of the East European communist states, Romania experienced the most brutal end of its regime. Violence broke out first in predomi-*

*nantly Hungarian regions of Transylvania and then in the capital of Bucharest before Nicolae Ceauşescu and his wife Elena fled the city. They were captured after several days and swiftly tried in front of a military tribunal, which immediately executed the dictator and his wife. The transcript, excerpted here, displays the depth of anger toward the Ceauşescus' dictatorship and also the leaders' megalomania and lack of comprehension regarding the opposition's grievances.*

---

*Prosecutor.* Please, make a note: Ceauşescu does not recognize the new legal structures of power of the country. He still considers himself to be the country's president and the commander in chief of the army.

Why did you ruin the country so much[?] Why did you export everything? Why did you make the peasants starve? The produce which the peasants grew was exported, and the peasants came from the most remote provinces to Bucharest and to the other cities in order to buy bread. They cultivated the soil in line with your orders and had nothing to eat. Why did you starve the people?

*Ceauşescu.* I will not answer this question. As a simple citizen, I tell you the following: For the first time I guaranteed that every peasant received 200 kilograms of wheat per person, not per family, and that he is entitled to more. It is a lie that I made the people starve. A lie, a lie in my face. This shows how little patriotism there is, how many treasonable offenses were committed.

*Prosecutor.* You claim to have taken measures so that every peasant is entitled to 200 kilograms of wheat. Why do the peasants then buy their bread in Bucharest?

[*The prosecutor quotes Ceauşescu, Ceauşescu's program.*]

*Prosecutor.* We have wonderful programs. Paper is patient. However, why are your programs not implemented? You have destroyed the Romanian villages and the Romanian soil. What do you say as a citizen?

*Ceauşescu.* As a citizen, as a simple citizen, I tell you the following: At no point was there such an upswing, so much construction, so much consolidation in the Romanian provinces. I guaranteed that every village has its schools, hospitals and doctors. I have done everything to create a decent and rich life for the people in the country, like in no other country in the world.

*Prosecutor.* We have always spoken of equality. We are all equal. Everybody should be paid according to his performance. Now we finally saw your villa on television, the golden plates from which you ate, the foodstuffs that you had imported, the luxurious celebrations, pictures from your luxurious celebrations.

*Elena Ceauşescu.* Incredible. We live in a normal apartment, just like every other citizen. We have ensured an apartment for every citizen through corresponding laws.

*Prosecutor.* You had palaces.

*Ceauşescu.* No, we had no palaces. The palaces belong to the people.

[*The prosecutor agrees, but stresses that they lived in them while the people suffered.*]

*Prosecutor.* Children cannot even buy plain candy, and you are living in the palaces of the people.

*Ceauşescu.* Is it possible that we are facing such charges?

*Prosecutor.* Let us now talk about the accounts in Switzerland, Mr. Ceausescu. What about the accounts?

*Elena Ceauşescu.* Accounts in Switzerland? Furnish proof!

*Ceauşescu.* We had no account in Switzerland. Nobody has opened an account. This shows again how false the charges are. What defamation, what provocations! This was a coup d'etat.

*Prosecutor.* Well, Mr. Defendant, if you had no accounts in Switzerland, will you sign a statement confirming that the money that may be in Switzerland should be transferred to the Romanian state, the State Bank.

*Ceauşescu.* We will discuss this before the Grand National Assembly. I will not say anything here. This is a vulgar provocation.

*Prosecutor.* Will you sign the statement now or not?

*Ceauşescu.* No, no. I have no statement to make, and I will not sign one.

*Prosecutor.* Note the following: The defendant refuses to sign this statement. The defendant has not recognized us. He also refuses to recognize the new forum.

*Ceauşescu.* I do not recognize this new forum.

*Prosecutor.* So you know the new forum. You have information about it.

[*Elena and Nicolae Ceauşescu state: Well, you told us about it. You told us about it here.*]

*Ceauşescu.* Nobody can change the state structures. This is not possible. Usurpers have been punished severely during the past centuries in Romania's history. Nobody has the right to abolish the Grand National Assembly.

[*The prosecutor turns to Elena: You have always been wiser and more ready to talk, a scientist. You were the most important aide, the number two in the cabinet, in the government.*]

*Prosecutor.* Did you know about the genocide in Timisoara?

*Elena Ceauşescu.* What genocide? By the way, I will not answer any more questions.

---

Available at http://www.ceausescu.org.

## DISCUSSION QUESTIONS

1. What crimes are the prosecution accusing the Ceauşescus of committing?
2. How do the Ceauşescus view themselves and their leadership in Romania?

# Václav Havel, New Year's Speech to the Nation (January 1, 1990)

*Dissident playwright and essayist turned politician, Václav Havel emerged as the undisputed leader of the Velvet Revolution in November 1989. He was elected the first noncommunist president in over four decades by the country's legislature, still controlled by the Communist Party. In his inaugural speech, excerpted here, Havel reflected on the historic legacy of the November revolution but also warned his citizens that the country faced tremendous challenges in the economy, the environment, and ethnic tensions.*

My dear fellow citizens, For forty years you heard from my predecessors on this day different variations on the same theme: how our country was flourishing, how many million tons of steel we produced, how happy we all were, how we trusted our government, and what bright perspectives were unfolding in front of us.

I assume you did not propose me for this office so that I, too, would lie to you.

Our country is not flourishing. The enormous creative and spiritual potential of our nation is not being used sensibly. Entire branches of industry are producing goods that are of no interest to anyone, while we are lacking the things we need. A state which calls itself a workers' state humiliates and exploits workers. Our obsolete economy is wasting the little energy we have available. A country that once could be proud of the educational level of its citizens spends so little on education that it ranks today as seventy-second in the world. We have polluted the soil, rivers and forests bequeathed to us by our ancestors, and we have today the most contaminated environment in Europe. Adults in our country die earlier than in most other European countries.

Allow me a small personal observation. When I flew recently to Bratislava, I found some time during discussions to look out of the plane window. I saw the industrial complex of Slovnaft chemical factory and the giant Petržalka housing estate right behind it. The view was enough for me to understand that for decades our statesmen and political leaders did not look or did not want to look out of the windows of their plane. No study of statistics available to me would enable me to understand faster and better the situation in which we find ourselves.

But all this is still not the main problem. The worst thing is that we live in a contaminated moral environment. We fell morally ill because we became used to saying something different from what we thought. We learned not to believe in anything, to ignore one another, to care only about ourselves. Concepts such as love, friendship, compassion, humility or forgiveness lost their depth and dimension, and for many of us they represented only psychological peculiarities, or they resembled gone-astray greetings from ancient times, a little ridiculous in the era of computers and spaceships. Only a few of us were able to cry out loudly that the powers that be should not be all-powerful and that the special farms, which produced ecologically pure and top-quality food just for them, should send their produce to schools, children's homes and hospitals if our agriculture was unable to offer them to all.

The previous regime—armed with its arrogant and intolerant ideology—reduced man to a force of production, and nature to a tool of production. In this it attacked both their very substance and their mutual relationship. It reduced gifted and autonomous people, skillfully working in their own country, to the nuts and bolts of some monstrously huge, noisy and stinking machine, whose real meaning was not clear to anyone. It could not do more than slowly but inexorably wear out itself and all its nuts and bolts.

When I talk about the contaminated moral atmosphere, I am not talking just about the gentlemen who eat organic vegetables and do not look out of the plane windows. I am talking about all of us. We had all become used to the totalitarian system and accepted it as an unchangeable fact and thus helped to perpetuate it. In other words, we are all—though naturally to differing extents—responsible for the operation of the totalitarian machinery. None of us is just its victim. We are all also its co-creators.

Why do I say this? It would be very unreasonable to understand the sad legacy of the last forty years as something alien, which some distant relative bequeathed to us. On the contrary, we have to accept this legacy as a sin we committed against ourselves. If we accept it as such, we will understand that it is up to us all, and up to us alone to do something about it. We cannot blame the previous rulers for everything, not only because it would be untrue, but also because it would blunt the duty that each of us faces today: namely, the obligation to act independently, freely, reasonably and quickly. Let us not be mistaken: the best government in the world, the best parliament and the best president, cannot achieve much on their own. And it would be wrong to expect a general remedy from them alone. Freedom and democracy include participation and therefore responsibility from us all.

If we realize this, then all the horrors that the new Czechoslovak democracy inherited will cease to appear so terrible. If we realize this, hope will return to our hearts.

In the effort to rectify matters of common concern, we have something to lean on. The recent period—and in particular the last six weeks of our peaceful revolution—has shown the enormous human, moral and spiritual potential, and the civic culture that slumbered in our society under the enforced mask of apathy. Whenever someone categorically claimed that we were this or that, I always objected that society is a very mysterious creature and that it is unwise to trust only the face it presents to you. I am happy that I was not mistaken. Everywhere in the world people wonder where those meek, humiliated, skeptical and seemingly cynical citizens of Czechoslovakia found the marvelous strength to shake the totalitarian yoke from their shoulders in several weeks, and in a decent and peaceful way. And let us ask: Where did the young people who never knew another system get their desire for truth, their love of free thought, their political ideas, their civic courage and civic prudence? How did it happen that their parents—the very generation that had been considered lost—joined them? How is it that so many people immediately knew what to do and none needed any advice or instruction?

I think there are two main reasons for the hopeful face of our present situation. First of all, people are never just a product of the external world; they are also able to relate themselves to something superior, however systematically the external world tries to kill that ability in them. Secondly, the humanistic and democratic traditions, about which there had been so much idle talk, did after all slumber in the unconsciousness of our nations and ethnic minorities, and were inconspicuously passed from one generation to another, so that each of us could discover them at the right time and transform them into deeds.

We had to pay, however, for our present freedom. Many citizens perished in jails in the 1950s, many were executed, thousands of human lives were destroyed, hundreds of thousands of talented people were forced to leave the country. Those who defended the honor of our nations during the Second World War, those who rebelled against totalitarian rule and those who simply managed to remain themselves and think freely, were all persecuted. We should not forget any of those who paid for our present freedom in one way or another. Independent courts should impartially consider the possible guilt of those who were responsible for the persecutions, so that the truth about our recent past might be fully revealed.

Václav Havel, *Open Letters: Selected Writings, 1965–1990* (New York: Alfred A. Knopf, 1991), 390–96.

## DISCUSSION QUESTIONS

1. Havel claims his country is not flourishing. What are his concerns as Czechoslovakia begins its new chapter?
2. What does Havel mean when he says that the moral landscape of Czechoslovakia is contaminated?
3. What does Havel believe are his main tasks as the country's new president?

## China Beijing Spring

# An Open Letter to Beijing University Authorities (April 3, 1989)

*Students saw Hu Yaobang as their most important champion for democratic reform in the party. His death on April 15 is generally seen as the start of the Tiananmen Square movement. However, this document, signed by Wang Dan (one of the eventual leaders of the protests) and fifty-five other students is dated April 4, showing that the movement for democracy was already in motion before Hu's death enabled it to take a higher profile. In this petition, the students are clearly tying their protests to a tradition of intellectual and student protest in China, particularly the May Fourth Movement. The May Fourth Movement of 1919 protested both foreign imperialism and China's weak government, and helped to advance the cause of student protest in China. May Fourth gave rise to an entire generation of intellectual protest, including the roots of the Communist Party. For this reason, May Fourth is seen as a vital date in China's revolutionary calendar, and the students of May Fourth are depicted on the Monument to Revolutionary Martyrs in Tiananmen Square, which became the focal point of the 1989 protests.*

---

President Ding Shisun, Party Secretary Wang Xuezhen, the University Party Committee, the Department of Student Affairs, and the University Youth League Committee:

This year marks the seventieth anniversary of the May Fourth Movement.[1] As the birthplace of this extraordinary movement of democratic enlightenment, Beijing University has always held high the banners of democracy and science [the two main rallying calls of the May Fourth Movement] and marched at the very forefront of our nation's progress. Today, as Chinese commemorate the May Fourth Movement, we, students of Beijing University, the hallowed ground of democracy, continue to hope that we will be able to carry on the distinguished tradition of Beijing University.

Thinking back seventy years, we recall how President Cai Yuanpei put the ideas of "democracy for governance of the school," freedom of thought, and tolerance of diversity into practice, fully ensuring that there would be academic freedom and freedom of speech within the school walls. Beijing University at that time could boast an unprecedented vitality in intellectual life, various scholarly trends, and many different schools of thought. In that environment, innumerable men and women of excellence, whose lives would later shine in the history of China, matured. This kind of democratic campus atmosphere still fills us with awe and pride. Yet we also note with great sorrow that today, seventy

---

[1] The May Fourth Movement, which spanned the years 1919 to 1921, was a broad movement both of student and intellectual political activism and of cultural reform. During this period, students and intellectuals initiated a nationalist, anti-imperialist campaign to strengthen China through modernization and social reform; their rallying cry was "Democracy and Science." Accompanying this political activism, which contributed to the birth of the Communist Party and other political organizations, was a vigorous literary and philosophical movement to embrace Western thought and reject traditional Chinese thinking and values. This period of social and cultural change is commonly referred to as the "May Fourth Movement," after historic student protests on May 4, 1919, against Chinese government capitulation to Japanese and other foreign powers' demands for colonial concessions. The movement still holds great meaning for Chinese students and intellectuals.

years later, this legacy of academic freedom and freedom of speech is in danger. One indication of this is the existence of many university restrictions regarding students' freedom to establish student associations, sponsor lectures, organize discussion meetings and salons, and other aspects of student freedom. We cannot help recognizing the fact that the "TOEFL School" [referring to students who spent all their free time studying for the Test of English as a Foreign Language, the standard test required of prospective foreign students at American universities] and "Mahjong School" [referring to students who spent their free time playing mahjong, the traditional Chinese game played with bamboo tiles and vaguely similar to gin rummy] are in vogue, and that business fever has suffocated all other interests. While there can be no doubt that this is the result of many social factors, it also is closely linked to the various kinds of restrictions on students' freedom of thought.

. . . It is our belief that seeking democracy requires more than opening one's mouth and yelling loudly; one must begin with concrete matters, . . . with matters that one has a stake in. Specifically speaking, we should begin by working hard to improve the democratic environment in school. It is our belief that in institutions of higher learning, such as Beijing University, there should be full freedom of speech and academic freedom. The unreasonable restrictions on these freedoms that have been imposed for various reasons should be abolished. Beijing University should serve as a special zone for promoting the democratization of politics; it should make a contribution to the progress of Chinese democracy.

We greatly treasure social and school stability and unity. Therefore, we would like to put forward the following suggestions, which stem from nothing other than a wish to establish channels for dialogue with the university leadership, from the desire to be open and honest with Party and Communist Youth League leaders of every level in the school, and to be treated likewise, and from our hope that with down-to-earth actions we can improve this learning environment of ours.

Beginning last semester and continuing today, from Activity Room 430 in Building 43 to the "democracy lawn" in front of the

statue of Cervantes, thirteen democracy salons have been spontaneously organized by students concerned with the future of the
country and the Chinese nation. These salons have provided the
students with excellent opportunities for the exchange of ideas as
well as for theoretical discussions. Recently, however, a few salons
have run into interference from the Beijing Municipal Party
Committee, the Party Committee of the University, the Security
Department, and the Party branch in every academic department.
Some students have also been personally subject to considerable
pressure from authorities. We believe that these salons offer an opportunity to explore spontaneously various ideas; such forums
greatly help to enliven the academic atmosphere and promote the
exchange of ideas. And it is the wish of the majority of students
to maintain the once-a-week democracy salons. Therefore, we
suggest:

(1) That the university take the initiative to remove all types of
pressure [on the students], lend its support to the sponsors of the
democracy salons and similar activities, and grant them the freedom to invite eminent scholars to participate.

(2) The freedom referred to above should be precisely defined
[by the following procedures]: two days in advance of a scheduled
democracy salon, the organizers of these spontaneous meetings will
furnish to university authorities for registration a list of the persons
invited. In turn, university authorities should guarantee that they
will permit all people to attend, with the exception of those who
have lost their political rights.[2]

(3) That the university designate the "democracy lawn" in front
of the statue of Cervantes as a regular meeting place for the democracy salons. The university may dispatch personnel to participate in the activities each time to help keep order, but this should
not be used as an excuse for interfering in the activities.

(4) That the university guarantee it will not take any measures
against the organizers of these spontaneous activities, that it will

---

[2]Articles 50–54 of the Criminal Law of the PRC [People's Republic of China] provides that
counter-revolutionaries and criminals convicted of serious crimes may be deprived of their
political rights (which include the right to vote and stand for election and to hold a leading
position in government offices, enterprises, or citizen's organizations), in addition to being
sentenced to imprisonment, public surveillance, or death.

not hold people responsible after the event, and that it will not prevent them from receiving their diplomas. . . .

We end this petition with the signatures that we have collected. We hereby appeal to all of the teachers and students of the university: please support our reasonable requests. We are confident that the wish to establish a real democracy first of all within the school campus is not the wish of only the signers of this petition, but also of all of the teachers and students. We therefore earnestly look forward to your support through your signatures.

> —Wang Dan and 55 other students,
> April 3, 1989
> *(big-character poster at*
> *Beijing University)*

Minzhu Han and Sheng Hua, eds., *Cries for Democracy: Writings and Speeches from the 1989 Chinese Democracy Movement* (Princeton, NJ: Princeton University Press, 1990), 16–19.

## DISCUSSION QUESTIONS

1. What were the students' goals in presenting these demands?
2. How is it significant that these demands were expressed prior to the start of demonstrations in Tiananmen Square?
3. How do these demands compare to the demands made by protesters in Eastern Europe?

# Nicholas Kristof, Obituary for Hu Yaobang (April 16, 1989)

*This obituary for Hu Yaobang outlines his life, including his downfall in 1987. In it can be seen many of the reasons the student movement seized on his death as an opportunity, including his sterling revolutionary credentials and his role in advocating reforms during the mid-1980s. The document also hints at the complicated reaction of the Chinese Communist Party toward Hu's death.*

Hu Yaobang, who helped navigate China away from orthodox Marxism and led the world's largest Communist Party for six years until he was forced to resign in disgrace in January 1987, died today, the Government announced. He was 73 years old.

The official New China News Agency said Mr. Hu died of complications from a heart attack suffered on April 8, when he reportedly collapsed during a Politburo meeting. The agency tonight distributed a glowing obituary of Mr. Hu, presumably at least in part to divert criticism that the party had mistreated him.

Mr. Hu's vigor and impetuousness carried him from a humble peasant family, which he left at age 14 to join the Communist guerrilla forces fighting in China's civil war, to the summit of power in the capital. And yet the same characteristics ultimately doomed him, for other officials chafed at his tendency to make startling statements without thinking them through or consulting his colleagues.

### Had Few Sacred Cows

Nothing was sacred to Mr. Hu, not the memory of Mao Zedong, not even chopsticks. On a trip to Inner Mongolia in 1984, he suggested that the Chinese might start using Western utensils.

"We should prepare more knives and forks, buy more plates and sit around the table to eat Chinese food in the Western style, that is, each from his own plate," he urged. "By doing so, we can avoid contagious diseases."

Mr. Hu dropped the idea after his startled colleagues reproached him for criticizing a Chinese way of life.

In a nation where caution is often prized, he was the exception. Mr. Hu was one of the first Chinese leaders to abandon the Mao suit in favor of jacket and tie. And when he was asked which of Mao's thoughts were applicable in China's efforts to modernize its economy, he is reported to have replied: "I think, none."

### Right Arm to Deng Xiaoping

Mr. Hu played a critical role in helping his long-time mentor, Deng Xiaoping, gain and consolidate power in the late 1970's. In the early- and mid-1980's, he was in charge of day-to-day matters during China's liberalization.

And yet his extraordinary career was overshadowed by its even more extraordinary end: the blur in December 1986 and January 1987 that included tumultuous student demonstrations, a torrent of criticisms against him by top-level officials, his resignation, and the subsequent campaign against "bourgeois liberalization," or Western democratic influences.

His resignation came to be a milestone in post-Mao China, for several reasons. It showed that resistance to rapid change and personal style was considerable, especially among "old revolutionaries" and military officials. And it upset the plans for an orderly succession under which Mr. Hu could have taken over from Mr. Deng as paramount leader, instead opening the way for the rise of more cautious officials like Li Peng, now Prime Minister.

## Resignation and Crackdown

The "resignation" of Mr. Hu and the subsequent crackdown seemed to harm the party's credibility and to bolster his own. He became viewed, particularly by intellectuals, as a man who refused to bend with the political winds and who had paid the price.

"I am not a man of iron," Mr. Hu was once reported to have said. "I am a man of passion, of flesh and blood." It was a fair assessment of a leader who was so focused on change and the future that he neglected his flank.

In the period in which he served as top official of the party, from 1981 to 1897, Mr. Hu was often in the shadow of Mr. Deng. Thomas Chan, a China scholar at the University of Hong Kong, noted that while he was outspoken, Mr. Hu never transcended the process of collective decision-making.

Still, as time went on and Mr. Deng began to withdraw from day-to-day management of the country, it was Mr. Hu as much as anyone who tugged China toward market economics and a more open political system. In some ways Mr. Hu seemed to resemble his mentor. Like Mr. Deng, Mr. Hu was barely five feet three inches tall, but fired with enormous energy and pragmatism.

**Criticism in the Military**

Associates in the party and the military criticized Mr. Hu for moving too fast toward the market and for his tolerance of dissidents. Even Mr. Deng turned against him after students began demonstrating in several cities and calling for greater democracy.

Mr. Hu was born in November 1915 in Liuyang City, Hunan Province, the remote south-central region of spicy food and rebellious farmers. His parents were poor peasants and as a child he apparently never attended school, although he later taught himself to read. He took part in his first rebellion at age 12, and at 14 he ran away from home to join the Communists.

In 1934 and 1935, Mr. Hu was one of the youngest participants in the legendary Long March, during which the Communist rebels fled on foot 6,000 miles from southeast China to their new base in northwest China. Later he became an army political officer and quickly impressed his superior, Mr. Deng. After the Communist victory, Mr. Hu followed Mr. Deng to Beijing and became head of the Communist Party's organization for young people.

After Mao Zedong launched the Cultural Revolution in 1966, Mr. Deng fell from power and Mr. Hu fell with him. His head was shaved and he was sent to the countryside to tend livestock. Mr. Deng was restored to power from 1973 to 1976, and Mr. Hu's career was resuscitated for that period. Then Mr. Deng and Mr. Hu were purged again in early 1976, near the end of the Cultural Revolution.


**A Landmark Meeting**

In 1977, after Mao died and the country was seeking new directions, Mr. Deng and Mr. Hu began a slow return. At a landmark Central Committee meeting at the end of 1978, Mr. Hu was not only named to the Politburo but also head of the party's organization and propaganda departments. Mr. Hu won influence and helped consolidate Mr. Deng's rise to preeminence. His own star was also soaring.

He was named General Secretary of the Party, and in 1981 he succeeded Hua Guofeng as Party Chairman, then the top position.

A year later his title was changed back to General Secretary and that became the highest post in the party.

His downfall came in January 1987, amid a flurry of secret meetings that are still not entirely understood. On Jan. 16, 1987, a somber television announcer read a statement that Mr. Hu had resigned after making "a self-criticism of his mistakes on major issues of political principles in violation of the party's principle of collective leadership."

Mr. Hu subsequently went into seclusion, and Beijing Review reported in 1988 that he spent his time reading reminiscences of China's revolutionary marshals, practicing calligraphy and walking long distances for exercise.

Mr. Hu is believed to be survived by his wife, Li Zhao, four children and numerous grandchildren.

*New York Times,* April 16, 1989.

## DISCUSSION QUESTIONS

1. What in Hu Yaobang's biography suggests his popularity with students and reformers?
2. What were Hu's major political and economic reforms?
3. Why was Hu controversial within the Communist Party, and why was he removed from power?

# *Renmin ribao (People's Daily)* **Editorial (April 26, 1989)**

*For many years, the Communist Party leadership indicated its opinions through editorials in the* People's Daily, *its official newspaper. The April 26 editorial was the government's first clear statement on the protests, after more than a week of uncertainty. The April 26 editorial condemned the demonstrations as the result of "a small handful of plotters" creating turmoil. The crowds were ordered to disperse under threat of martial law. The April 26 editorial was a crucial moment in the protest: "turmoil" (*dongluan) *was a politically charged term, often referring to the chaos of the cultural revolution, and by accusing the* *students of instigating turmoil, the government was declaring them counter-revolutionary and thus liable to be suppressed by the government. The protest that had begun to mourn a party official and submit grievances to the government leader had become an act of defiance.*

*The editorial clearly labeled the protests as counter-revolutionary and accused "a small handful" of instigating chaos. From this point forward, one of the main goals of the students and their supporters was the reversal of the judgment of the April 26 editorial.*

---

In their activities to mourn the death of Comrade Hu Yaobang, communists, workers, peasants, intellectuals, cadres, members of the People's Liberation Army and young students have expressed their grief in various ways. They have also expressed their determination to turn grief into strength to make contributions in realizing the four modernizations and invigorating the Chinese nation.

Some abnormal phenomena have also occurred during the mourning activities. Taking advantage of the situation, an extremely small number of people spread rumors, attacked party and state leaders by name, and instigated the masses to break into the Xinhua Gate at Zhongnanhai, where the party Central Committee and the State Council are located. Some people even shouted such reactionary slogans as, Down with the Communist Party. In Xi'an and Changsha, there have been serious incidents in which some lawbreakers carried out beating, smashing, looting, and burning.

Taking into consideration the feelings of grief suffered by the masses, the party and government have adopted an attitude of tolerance and restraint toward some improper words uttered and actions carried out by the young students when they were emotionally agitated. On April 22, before the memorial meeting was held, some students had already show[n] up at Tiananmen Square, but they were not asked to leave, as they normally would have been. Instead, they were asked to observe discipline and join in the mourning for Comrade Hu Yaobang. The students on the square were themselves able to consciously maintain order. [Beijing Xinhua Domestic Service in Chinese at 1400 GMT on April 25, reporting on the April 26 *Renmin ribao* editorial, deletes this sentence.] Owing to the joint efforts by all concerned, it was possible for the memorial meeting to proceed in a solemn and respectful manner.

However, after the memorial meeting, an extremely small number of people with ulterior purposes continued to take advantage of the young students' feelings of grief for Comrade Hu Yaobang to spread all kinds of rumors to poison and confuse people's minds. Using both big- and small-character posters, they vilified, hurled invectives at, and attacked party and state leaders. Blatantly violating the Constitution, they called for opposition to the leadership by the Communist Party and the socialist system. In some of the institutions of higher learning, illegal organizations were formed to seize power from the student unions. In some cases, they even forcibly took over the broadcasting systems on the campuses. In some institutions of higher learning, they instigated the students and teachers to go on strike and even went to the extent of forcibly preventing students from going to classes, usurped the name of the workers' organizations to distribute reactionary handbills, and established ties everywhere in an attempt to create even more serious incidents.

These facts prove that what this extremely small number of people did was not to join in the activities to mourn Comrade Hu Yaobang or to advance the course of socialist democracy in China. Neither were they out to give vent to their grievances. Flaunting the banner of democracy, they undermined democracy and the legal system. Their purpose was to sow dissension among the people, plunge the whole country into chaos and sabotage the political situation of stability and unity. This is a planned conspiracy and a disturbance. Its essence is to, once and for all, negate the leadership of the CPC [Chinese Communist Party] and the socialist system. This is a serious political struggle confronting the whole party and the people of all nationalities throughout the country.

If we are tolerant of or conniving with this disturbance and let it go unchecked, a seriously chaotic state will appear. Then, the reform and opening up; the improvement of the economic environment and the rectification of the economic order, construction, and development; the control over prices; the improvement of our living standards; the drive to oppose corruption; and the development of democracy and the legal system expected by the people throughout the country, including the young students, will all become empty hopes. Even the tremendous achievements scored in the reform during the past decade may be completely lost, and the great aspiration of the revitalization of China cherished by the whole nation will be hard to realize. A China with very good prospects and a very bright future will become a chaotic and unstable China without any future.

The whole party and the people nationwide should fully understand the seriousness of this struggle, unite to take a clear-cut stand to oppose the disturbance, and firmly preserve the hard-earned situation of political stability and unity, the Constitution, socialist democracy, and the legal system. Under no circumstances should the establishment of any illegal organizations be allowed. It is imperative to firmly stop any acts that use any excuse to infringe upon the rights and interests of legitimate organizations of students. Those who have deliberately fabricated rumors and framed others should be investigated to determine their criminal liabilities according to law. Bans should be placed on unlawful parades and demonstrations and on such acts as going to factories, rural areas, and schools to establish ties. Beating, smashing, looting, and burning should be punished according to law. It is necessary to protect the just rights of students to study in class. The broad masses of students sincerely hope that corruption will be eliminated and democracy will be promoted. These, too, are the demands of the party and the government. These demands can only be realized by strengthening the efforts for improvement and rectification, vigorously pushing forward the reform, and making perfect our socialist democracy and our legal system under the party leadership.

All comrades in the party and the people throughout the country must soberly recognize the fact that our country will have no peaceful days if this disturbance is not checked resolutely. This struggle concerns the success or failure of the reform and opening up, the program of the four modernizations, and the future of our state and nation. Party organizations of the CPC at all levels, the broad masses of members of the Communist Party and the Communist Youth League, all democratic parties, and patriotic democratic personages, and the people around the country should make a clear distinction between right and wrong, take positive action, and struggle to firmly and quickly stop the disturbance.

Beijing Domestic Service, reported 0930 Greenwich Mean Time, April 25; Foreign Broadcast Information Service, April 25, pp. 23–24.

## DISCUSSION QUESTIONS

1. How does the editorial characterize the protests (including their participants, motives, tactics, and goals)? What does it describe as the relationship between the protesters and democracy?
2. Why is this editorial so dangerous to the protesters?
3. What does the editorial propose as the proper response to the protests?

# Open Letter to the Central Committee of the Chinese Communist Party (April 28, 1989)

*This document is a poster displayed on the square and signed by a student from Wuhan. It is clearly a response to the April 26 editorial and is remarkably moderate in its tone. Although it is strident in expressing the need for reform, it is also consistent in trying to make clear to the government that the verdict of the April 26 editorial is incorrect because the students represent part of the same revolutionary tradition as the Communist Party itself.*

Honorable members of the Central Committee of the Chinese Communist Party, the State Council, and the Standing Committee of the National People's Congress:

We are very pleased that you have not taken harsh measures against the students marching and petitioning in Tiananmen Square. However, what right do you have to act otherwise? What right do you have to label the actions that students rightfully take to show their concern for the welfare of the country and its people "illegal activities incited and participated in by a small handful of bad people who aim to destroy the stability and unity of our country"? We think you must be aware that the people who have participated in the "events" are by no means "a small handful," nor are they only students from Beijing. Students in Shanghai, Wuhan, Jinan, and other medium- and large-sized cities have also taken to the streets at the same time. How can it be that a "small handful" of people have the influence to manipulate the entire country's students? No, we certainly have not been used by others. We act completely of our own accord! We act out of a true love of our Motherland and the Chinese nation! Our fervent hearts and our consciences do not allow us to keep silent any longer. We must rise up and come to the rescue of our homeland, which is afflicted with a multitude of ills.

At each student movement, the government invokes the same old refrain: "We must maintain a stable and unified political situation. . . ." In comparison to countries like Iran, Iraq, Israel, and Haiti, our country is stable and unified. Yet why doesn't the government use the dialectical method (of which Mao often reminded us) of "dividing into two" the great "whole," that is, why can't it see the other side of this heralded "situation of stability and unity"? If it did, then perhaps it would be able to grasp the problems facing our country. I feel that using the expression "rot coated with gold and jade" to describe the country's present situation is rather apt. Let us take a look at our country.

Officialdom is a stretch of blackness. Using the expression, "out of ten officials, nine are corrupt" to describe the situation of every level of the bureaucracy in our country is no exaggeration. This is especially true of cadres at the grass-roots level. They are "hick" emperors; during their term of office, the people have suffered, their waists growing narrower as officials' waists thicken. The forerunner of the Chinese democratic revolution, Sun Yat-sen, held that officials are supposed to be the "servants of the people," but what we have now is exactly the opposite.[1] Foreign presidents who come to our country are bewildered by the sight of police cars opening up a path for our state cadres when they venture out. Let's see what these foreign guests have to say: "Our people are the taxpayers, we all depend on them for our living, we dare not make the people yield the road to us." Perhaps some will say that this is false humility on their part, designed to win the people's support. But what about us? We are incapable of anything, even this type of "hypocrisy." A good portion of cadres only know how to issue decrees and orders, to attend endless banquets, to squander the wealth created by the people's sweat and blood, to cram the gold of the national treasury into their pockets, so swollen that no more can be stuffed in. Profiteering by government officials, bureaucratism, officials protecting one another . . . these phenomena are not unlike hordes of termites rotting the foundation of the socialist tower and invading the body of our motherland.

Our society is a mess. It has fallen into its most serious plight since Liberation.[2] Murder, violence, and robbery have become the norm rather than the exception. People who see others in danger do not go to their rescue. People who see money instead open their eyes and forget all else. . . . How many citizens are there who do not even possess a minimal level of morality? This only demonstrates that our country's laws are weak and ineffective, and that the government is incompetent. . . .

The contributions of the Chinese Communist Party to the Chinese revolution are undeniable, despite its errors. During the period of war [when the Party first joined the battle against the Japanese invaders and then liberated the Chinese from the corrupt rule of the

[1] Sun Yat-sen, often referred to as "father of the country," is a towering figure in both Communist Chinese and Guomindang versions of modern Chinese history. While in exile, Sun founded the Revolutionary Alliance (Tongmeng Hui), which launched a series of domestic revolts against the Manchu throne from 1905 to 1911. Although the roles of Sun and the Revolutionary Alliance in the Revolution of 1911, which finally precipitated the abdication of the emperor, has been disputed by some historians, Sun was indisputably a leading figure in the revolutionary movement of the 1920s that sought to end the rule of warlords and unite China. In fundraising speeches in the United States after the suppression of the Democracy Movement, top Chinese dissidents, heedful of strong anticommunist sentiment among many Chinese-Americans, but also clearly willing to cast themselves in the role of inheritors of Sun's revolutionary legacy, repeatedly quoted Sun—not Mao Zedong.

[2] In Communist Chinese parlance, "Liberation" is the Communist liberation of China in 1949 from Guomindang rule and oppression.

Guomindang], the people loved and supported the Party because it indeed brought the people benefits. But history has moved forward. Now as we approach the end of the twentieth century, what is the situation of the Party? It may be said that a great portion of the people no longer trust the Party. The reason for this is not a small handful of people who, wanting to overturn the rule of the Communist Party, spread rumors throughout the masses; rather, it is the corruption of the Party itself. Is the governance of the pyramid—the elaborate Party organization with its levels and levels—serving a positive or negative function? The peasants hate most the local county Party secretaries, for they are incapable of doing anything other than extorting money earned with the peasants' blood and sweat and gorging themselves until they are fat and their faces greasy and shiny. As for the workers, the faces they abhor most are those of the secretaries of the factories' Party Committees, because they only know how to preach lectures at endless meetings; they have neither the ability nor the knowledge to discuss technical matters. And as for university students, they dislike most those "administrators" [Party officials in the schools], because the only know how to conduct, gesticulating absurdly, "political study" classes.[3] If the entire society voices dissatisfaction with this stratum of officials who only feed themselves from the bowls the Party has secured for them without doing any work, the Secretary General of the Party should consider how to put an end to such a state of affairs.

The nature of the relationship between the Party and people is the same as the nature of the relationship between the army and the people. Just as fish cannot survive without water, the Party cannot survive without the people.[4] It was the people who created the

[3] "Political study" classes are study sessions called and led by Party officials during which Marxist theory, the Party's recent policies, and important speeches by leaders are studied and discussed. In the 1980s, under Deng Xiaoping's policy of emphasizing economic development over class struggle and politics, political study sessions steadily became less regular. At leading universities such as Beijing University and People's University, most departments held study sessions only once every several weeks, whereas they had been held at least once a week during the late 1970s and virtually every day during the Cultural Revolution. In recent years a typical session would begin with the Party official reading portions of speeches or editorials from the *People's Daily* and soliciting comments. Discussion was often lethargic and extremely superficial; most persons at the sessions can best be described as apathetic. Since the suppression of the Democracy Movement, political study sessions have been revived.

[4] A famous saying by Mao Zedong described the relationship between the Communist army and the people as that of "fish and water."

Party and who made the Party's ranks grow. It is the people who raise and sustain several million soldiers and several hundred million cadres, big and small alike. But for a long time now, the Party has put its interests and influence ahead of the government and the state; for a long time, it has touted itself as the "great Party," the "glorious Party," and the "correct Party." In its absolute rectitude and perfection, it calls on the people to "keep step with the Party Central Committee," and orders the people "to conscientiously carry out and implement the policies and decisions of the Central Committee" (regardless of whether they are correct or not). Whoever dares to raise a dissenting opinion is considered anti-Party and "anti-socialist." For these people, the Party does not hesitate to pick on their personal faults or problems, bludgeon them, or brand them with political labels. Do not believe that this type of thing only occurred during the Cultural Revolution. In 1987, there was Fang Lizhi, Liu Binyan, and Wang Ruowang; most recently, the investigation of and intervention in the *Science and Technology Daily* and the Shanghai *World Economic Herald* (two papers read by intellectuals).[5] The authorities' suppression of the students' constitutionally valid activities in Beijing and the use of electric prods on students by the Wuhan police—what are the differences between these incidents and the measures used in the Cultural Revolution against intellectuals, or the measures used by the Guomindang in the late 1930s to repress student movements? If the Communist Party truly represents the interests of the people, the people will follow the Party without hesitation. But if the Party formulates policies that are inappropriate to China's situation, and issues mistaken orders, must

---

[5] Liu Binyan (an investigative journalist), Wang Ruowang (a writer), and Fang Lizhi were three outspoken liberal intellectuals expelled from the Party in the Anti-Bourgeois Liberalism campaign in 1987. Fang, a respected astrophysicist and vociferous critic of the Party who has openly challenged the merits of Marxism, was made one of the main scapegoats for the 1986 student unrest. Liu is best known for his pioneering pieces of "reportage literature," candid exposés of Party corruption and malfeasance, published in the late 1970s and early 1980s. He is currently residing in the United States, and in 1989 was one of the founding members of the Federation for a Democratic China . . . Wang Ruowang, a prominent figure in Shanghai intellectual circles, was labeled a bourgeois liberal for his criticism of the Party and its monopoly on power. In September 1989 he was arrested; he has since been accused of writing articles in support of the student protests and giving "counter-revolutionary" speeches in People's Square in Shanghai.

the people still follow? The Party is not a god; nor is it a one-person organization. Yet, the Party has deified itself. . . .

In recent years the Party has changed to become more courageous than in the past. It is beginning to acknowledge th[at] "nobody can be correct forever, the Party too is infallible, and therefore making mistakes is permissible." Indeed, whether committed by persons or by the Party, mistakes are unavoidable. This is obvious in the Party's past decisions to ignore population control, to initiate the Cultural Revolution, and to criticize, denounce, and ostracize our country's intellectuals. But these have gone beyond mere mistakes; they are crimes—against all of the people and against the entire Chinese nation! According to law, those guilty of murder must be sentenced to capital punishment. The consequence of the Party's crimes is not only the death of one or two persons, or a dozen or so people, but a threat to the existence of our entire state and our entire nation!

Yet no one has assigned guilt to Mao Zedong or to the Party. This is perhaps because our legal system is not sound, and our society is governed by the whim of the powerful. Despite the fact that we now have an established legal system, the Party remains paramount. The fact that when Party members commit crimes, Party discipline instead of law is used to sanction them is irrefutable evidence of this.[6]

---

[6] Disciplinary Inspection Committees established at all but the lowest levels of the Party hierarchy are responsible for investigating and disciplining Party members accused of violating Party discipline or breaking the law. Article 39 of the Party's charter provides for five types of punishment: (1) a warning; (2) a serious warning; (3) dismissal from Party posts and a recommendation to non-Party organizations to dismiss the wayward person from non-Party posts; (4) placement on probation; and (5) expulsion from the Party.

Party members who are suspected of having committed a crime are afforded special protection from legal prosecution by a number of factors. First, Party procedures call for a Party investigation before the matter is turned over to the police or procurator. Only after the Party Disciplinary Inspection Committee has concluded that the member has committed the crime and has stripped him of his Party credentials will the police or procuratorate step in to take the case. Because the Secretary of a Disciplinary Inspection Committee is subordinate to the Secretary of the general Party Committee at the same level, it is nearly impossible for him to carry out an investigation of the party Committee Secretary or any persons the latter is shielding. Second, the "revolutionary record" of Party members or the fact that they have already been disciplined within the Party often mitigates the severity of legal punishment. Finally, courts will routinely consult with the Party Committee of the work unit of a convicted member before sentencing him.

Heraclitus of ancient Greece once said that "Man must fight for law, and be armed with the law in his struggles." During the Qin Dynasty, the great reformist Shang Yang[7] stated much the same. The point is that even ancient men realized the importance of law in governing a country. But, what is the present state of our legal system? Everywhere we see law replaced by power. For example, when a mayor's son breaks the law, he is not punished by the law, but by a private letter written by a provincial governor. This is the way all criminal activities committed by officials and their relatives are dealt with. Consequently, we have two systems for dealing with those who break the law—one for the average citizen, and one for Party members and their families. Furthermore, it is often the case that those who knowingly break the law go free if they have power, and often go on to punish the innocent. For those with power, good wine and cigarettes are effective problem solvers. And when a man has entered the circles of power, life suddenly becomes much easier for his friends and relatives as well. Although each year brings a plethora of new laws, the citizen is left wondering which should be taken seriously. Two thousand years ago, Shang Yang emphasized that "righteousness is important, but the law is even more important." He stressed that law should be applied without discrimination, regardless of an individual's status. Our forefathers understood the importance of law. . . .

However, the situation under our current system of law is quite different. The person who embezzles two hundred million yuan escapes the law because of his so-called contribution to the revolution. Consequently, the credibility of our system of law is seriously undermined. . . .

This is our "stable and unified" homeland! This "stable and unified" political situation is nothing but an exchange market for greedy officials and crooked clerks, an environment that generates official and private profiteers. It is a "stable and unified" one-party totalitarian government. Its continuation will surely lead to further corruption in our politics, and eventually to the country's damna-

---

[7] Shang Yang (d. 338 B.C.) was a statesman and one of the earliest Legalists, men who believed that strong laws were essential to effective governance. Their advocacy of a strong, impartial legal system was not rooted in the desire to protect individual rights, however, but in the goal of enabling a ruler to maintain control over local populations.

tion. What is there in this kind of "stability" and "unity" for us to value and fear losing?

The economic reform, though it promises some short-term achievements, does not offer fundamental solutions to the problems that ail our nation. Today and yesterday, in and out of China, one finds virtually no case where social reform depending entirely on changes of the economic structure of a given country has succeeded. China today faces a turning point in her history: it has been proven that the fossilized theoretical models derived from the classic works of Marx and Lenin, coupled with an imported political and economic system from the USSR, cannot bring prosperity to our country. But our country cannot turn to "complete Westernization."

The economic reforms that we have undertaken in the past ten years have left us worse off rather than better off; and the more reforms are proposed, the stronger resistance they meet, for the people's patience is nearly tried to its limit. The people remain tolerant not only because it is their well-trained habit to do so—a virtue much valued for centuries—but also because they understand that the current reforms are meant to bring them a better life. They hope for a speedy solution to the problems that currently afflict our society. However, their tolerance is after all not endless. The past ten years of experience have made it clear that economic reform alone will not work, and that it is imperative to reform our political system. However, as political reform necessarily threatens the interests of the big shots as well as those of the middle-level cadres between the big shots and the common people, its implementation entails great risks. The very thought that this group of top and minor officials, if they feel cornered, might act in unison to launch a second Cultural Revolution is a realistic threat for those who have had the taste of the cowsheds [makeshift prisons] in the Cultural Revolution. It is no wonder that policy makers have been reluctant to promote political reform.

It has been said that "the establishment of democracy is a long and gradual process." This much we understand; yet we insist on asking: isn't forty years long enough? and, after these past forty years, what stage is Chinese "democracy" at? We have nothing, virtually nothing—except the legacy of our idolization of Mao Zedong, whose "one line" could change the world; the legacy of branding those who loved our country, and who dared to speak out, "rightists" and "counter-revolutionaries"; the legacy of the Cultural Revolution, which condemned our nation to hell; and the legacy of expropriating the political rights of those who call for democracy. At street corners, one often hears people say that the reason the people in power bear so much fear and hatred toward democracy is that democracy threatens to take away their authority and monopoly of power. As students in modern times, we did not believe such talk, but placed our trust in the government. We held great expectations for the Party and the government—but now we must face cold reality: the government and the Party have always let us down!

China simply has too many problems, and I will name no more. I also realize that, either in theoretical training or in practical experience, I have no more wisdom than does our current leadership, even less than our Party. I express these personal viewpoints simply as a Chinese citizen, and as one of the millions of college students. I have a loyal and patriotic heart, and I long for our country's prosperity and strength. Perhaps the statements I have made above sound deviant and radical, and perhaps some will incur denunciation as "counter-revolutionary statements" for which I may even be put in jail. But as I believe, at least for now, that what I have written are the right, patriotic things to say, and will be beneficial to our country. I hope that my words will reach the desks of Premier Li Peng, Secretary General Zhao Ziyang, and Senior Deng.

It is my hope that our senior leaders will go more often to visit the factories and the schools, the countryside and the army, not only because there are many problems demanding their attention but also because only there will they find the key to the solutions that will save China from imminent disaster.

Youth are the backbone of China!

> —A student in the Auditing Department,
> Institute of Economics, Wuhan
> University, April 28, 1989
> *(small-character poster)*

Minzhu Han and Sheng Hua, eds., *Cries for Democracy: Writings and Speeches from the 1989 Chinese Democracy Movement* (Princeton, NJ: Princeton University Press, 1990), 50–57.

## DISCUSSION QUESTIONS

1. Based on your reading of this document, are the student protesters opposing or supporting the Chinese Communist Party?
2. What are the goals of the protest movement?
3. How does this document characterize Chinese history since 1949? Since 1979?

# Zhao Ziyang, Speech to Asian Development Bank (May 4, 1989)

*Even after the publication of the April 26 editorial, the Chinese leadership remained divided. Within the Communist Party, Zhao Ziyang was the most prominent supporter of reform and the students' strongest advocate. This speech shows that Zhao still maintained hope that the protests could be resolved without the use of force and that the April 26 editorial did not represent the opinion of everyone in the government or the party leadership. Excerpts of the speech are presented here.*

I believe the basic attitude of the great majority of the student demonstrators is one of both satisfaction and dissatisfaction with the Communist Party and the government. These students do not oppose our underlying system, but they do demand that we eliminate the flaws in our work. They are satisfied with our achievements in reform and construction over the past decade, as well as with the nation's general development. But they are irritated by mistakes we have made along the way. They are calling on us to correct those mistakes and to improve our work style, and these calls in fact correspond nicely with positions of the Party and the government, which are also to affirm our accomplishments and to correct our mistakes.

Are there attempts to exploit the student movement, and is such exploitation going on now? China is so huge that there are always going to be at least some people who want to see us in turmoil.

There will always be people ready to exploit our students, and they will miss no opportunity to do so. Such people are very few, but we must always be on guard against them. I am confident that the great majority of the students will see this point. Demonstrations are continuing in Beijing and elsewhere, but I have no doubt that the situation is going to calm down gradually and that China will be spared any major turmoil.

We should meet the students' reasonable demands through democracy and law, should be willing to reform, and should use rational and orderly methods. Let us put this more concretely: What most bothers the students right now is the scourge of corruption. But the Party and government have been working on this problem in recent years, so why are there so many voices of complaint, and why are they so loud? There are two reasons, I believe. One is that our flawed legal system and out lack of democratic supervision allow corruption to rage ou[t] of control. The other is that our lack of openness and transparency leads to rumors, inaccurate accusations, wild exaggerations, and outright fabrications about what the Party and government are doing. Most Party and government workers in fact live on low wages and have no income beyond their fixed salaries, let alone any legally sanctioned privileges. Yes, there are people who skirt the law, who grab special privileges; but there are fewer of them, and they do less harm, than people think. Of course the problem of corruption has to be solved, but that has to happen—can only happen—through reforms such as perfecting the legal system, improving democratic supervision, and increasing transparency.

And these same principles apply to how we should deal with the student demonstrations themselves. We need to use democracy and law and to reason in an atmosphere of order. We need to use dialogue to consult broadly with students, workers, intellectuals, members of the democratic parties, and citizens from all parts of society. We must exchange ideas and promote mutual understanding through democracy and law in an atmosphere of reason and order, working together to solve problems that concern everyone.

What we need most right now is calm, reason, self-restraint, and order as we move to solve problems through democracy and law. If the Party and government are willing to proceed in this way, I am confident that students and other segments of society will also find this to be the best way.

[Zhao's speech before the board of the ADB (Asian Development Bank) had been drafted by Bao Tong but, unlike his speech commemorating May Fourth, had not been discussed by the Politburo Standing Committee or sanctioned by the Central Secretariat. Zhao felt good about the speech before he delivered it, and nearly everything he heard afterward was positive.

Later in the day Li Peng had a private conversation with Zhao about the speech:][1]

*Li Peng.* "That was an excellent speech, Comrade Ziyang, and the response has been very positive. I'll echo you when I meet with the Asian Development Bank delegates tomorrow."

*Zhao Ziyang.* "I tried to set a mild tone. I hope it'll do some good in quieting the student movement down and in strengthening foreign investors' confidence in China's stability. . . . Comrade Li Peng, when I got back from North Korea I heard about the strong reactions to the April 26 editorial in the *People's Daily*. It seems to have turned into a real sore point that has the students all stirred up. Do you see any way to turn things around and calm them down?"

*Li Peng.* "Comrade Ziyang, as you know, the editorial reflected the spirit of the April 24 Politburo meeting, particularly the views of Comrade Xiaoping. There may be problems of tone here and there, but we can't possibly change the core message."

*Zhao Ziyang.* "Let me tell you how I see all this. I think the student movement has two important characteristics. First, the students' slogans call for things like supporting the Constitution, promoting democracy, and fighting corruption. These demands all echo positions of the Party and the government. Second, a great many people from all parts of society are out there joining the demonstrations and backing the students. And it's not just Beijing that's flooded with protesters; it's the same story in Shanghai, Tianjin,

---

[1] Account of conversation drawn from *Materials for the Fourth Plenum of the Thirteenth Central Committee*, "Remarks of Comrade Zhao Ziyang," Secretariat of the Fourth Plenum of the CCP Thirteenth Central Committee, June 23–24, 1989; and from Li Peng, "Report on mistakes committed by Comrade Zhao Ziyang during the anti-Party antisocialist turmoil," report to the Fourth Plenum of the Thirteenth Central Committee, June 23.

and other major cities. This has grown into a nationwide protest. I think the best way to bring the thing to a quick end is to focus on the mainstream views of the majority. My problem with the April 26 editorial is that it sets the mainstream aside and makes a general, all-encompassing pronouncement that the majority just can't accept; it generates an us-versus-them mentality. I have no quarrel with the view that a handful of people oppose the Four Basic Principles and are fishing in troubled waters. I said that in my speech today. But it's hard to explain, and also hard to believe, how hundreds of thousands of people all over the country could be manipulated by a tiny minority. The students feel stigmatized by the April 26 editorial, and that's the main thing that's set them off. I think we should revise the editorial, soften its tone a bit.'"

*Li Peng.* "The origins of this protest are complex, Comrade Ziyang. The editorial did not accuse the vast majority of students of creating turmoil. When Yuan Mu had his dialogue with the students, and again when he spoke with journalists, he explained the government's position several times over. The students should be quite clear about this by now. The trouble is, there's no sign the protests are subsiding. In fact, quite the opposite: Now we have illegal student organizations that are openly pressuring the government. You've read the petition from that 'AFS,' so you know they're trying to squeeze out the legal student organizations. And not just that: They want to negotiate with the Party and government as equals. They even add a lot of conditions, as if they're above the government. That petition of theirs was itself a threat. The elder comrades like Xiaoping, Chen Yun, and Xiannian are all convinced that a tiny minority of people are manipulating this protest from behind the scenes. Their purpose is quite clear: They want to negate the leadership of the CCP and negate the entire socialist system. I agree with our Elder comrades. And that's why I hold to the view that the April 26 editorial is accurate and cannot be changed."

*Zhao Ziyang.* "I'm not opposed to the term 'turmoil' in the editorial. But I believe that this refers only to the scale of the protest and to the degree to which it has affected social order and that it does not foreclose the question of the political nature of the protest—I mean whether it's spontaneous or antagonistic. I think we should publish another editorial distinguishing the majority of students and sympathizers from the tiny minority who are using the movement to fish in troubled waters, to create conflicts, and to attack the Party and socialism. That way we can avoid a sweeping characterization of the protests as an antagonistic conflict. We can concentrate on policies of persuasion and guidance and avoid the sharpening of conflict. This kind of approach is the best way to help calm the situation."

Li Peng; "I disagree, Comrade Ziyang."

In *The Tiananmen Papers* (New York: Public Affairs Press, 2001), 115–18.

## DISCUSSION QUESTIONS
1. To what causes does Zhao Ziyang attribute the demonstrations in Tiananmen Square?
2. How does he propose that the Chinese government respond?
3. How does this position differ from the government's eventual response to the protests? How do you account for the changes?

# New May Fourth Manifesto (May 4, 1989)

*This document, read aloud by Wu'er Kaixi, makes explicit the links between the 1989 protests and those of May 4, 1919, when students protested foreign imperialism and government weakness, urging the creation of a strong Chinese state that could protect the interests of its people against the predation of foreign powers.*

Fellow students, fellow countrymen:

Seventy years ago today, a large group of illustrious students assembled in front of Tiananmen, and a new chapter in the history of China was opened. Today, we are once again assembled here, not only to commemorate that monumental day but more importantly, to carry forward the May Fourth spirit of science and democracy. Today, in front of the symbol of the Chinese nation,

Tiananmen, we can proudly proclaim to all the people in our nation that we are worthy of the pioneers of seventy years ago.

For over one hundred years, the pioneers of the Chinese people have been searching for a path to modernize an ancient and beleaguered China. Following the Paris Peace Conference, they did not collapse in the face of imperialist oppression, but marched boldly forward.[1] Waving the banners of science and democracy, they launched the mighty May Fourth Movement. May Fourth and the subsequent New Democratic Revolution were the first steps in the patriotic democracy movement of Chinese students. From this point on, Chinese history entered a completely new phase. Due to the socioeconomic conditions in China and the shortcomings of intellectuals, the May Fourth ideals of science and democracy have not been realized. Seventy years of history have taught us that democracy and science cannot be established in one fell swoop and that impatience and despair are of no avail. In the context of China's economy and culture, the Marxism espoused by the Chinese Communist Party cannot avoid being influenced by remnants of feudal ideology. Thus, while New China has steadily advanced toward modernization, it has greatly neglected building a democracy.[2] Although it has emphasized the role of science, it has not valued the spirit of science—democracy. At present, our country is plagued with problems such as a bloated government bureaucracy, serious corruption, the devaluation of intellectual work, and inflation, all of which severely impede us from intensifying the reforms and carrying out modernization. This illustrates that if the spirit of science and democracy, and their actual processes, do not

---

[1] The "Paris Peace Conference" was the Versailles Peace Conference held in 1919 by the five allies (the United States, Great Britain, France, Italy, and Japan) after the defeat of Germany in World War I. As the conference began, many Chinese people, including intellectuals and students, expected that Germany's colonial claims in China, and particularly its claim to a large portion of Shandong Province under a ninety-nine-year lease forced on the Chinese government in 1898, would be annulled. The Chinese delegation's acceptance of an agreement between the Five Powers under which Japan took over Germany's colonial rights set off a bitter storm of protest in China, and was the immediate cause of the May Fourth Incident in which students protested in Tiananmen.

[2] "New China" is the term introduced by the Party to refer to the new republic founded in 1949, and appears in the names of some official organizations such as the New China News Agency (Xinhua News Agency).

exist, numerous and varied feudal elements and remnants of the old system, which are fundamentally antagonistic to large-scale socialist production, will reemerge in society, and modernization will be impossible. For this reason, carrying on the May Fourth spirit, hastening the reform of the political system, protecting human rights, and strengthening rule by law have become urgent tasks of modernization that we must undertake.

Fellow students, fellow countrymen, a democratic spirit is precisely the absorption of the collective wisdom of the people, the true development of each individual's ability, and the protection of each individual's interests; a scientific spirit is precisely respect for individual nature, and the building of the country on the basis of science. Now more than ever, we need to review the experiences and lessons of all student movements since May Fourth, to make science and rationalism a system, a process. Only then can the tasks the May Fourth Movement set before us be accomplished, only then can the spirit of May Fourth be carried forward, and only then can our wish for a strong China be realized.

Fellow students, fellow countrymen, the future and fate of the Chinese nation are intimately linked to each of our hearts. This student movement has but one goal, that is, to facilitate the process of modernization by raising high the banners of democracy and science, by liberating people from the constraints of feudal ideology, and by promoting freedom, human rights, and rule by law. To this end, we urge the government to accelerate the pace of political reform, to guarantee the rights of the people vested in the law, to implement a press law, to permit privately run newspapers, to eradicate corruption, to hasten the establishment of an honest and democratic government, to value education, to respect intellectual work, and to save the nation through science. Our views are not in conflict with those of the government. We only have one goal: the modernization of China.

. . . Our present tasks are: first, to take the lead in carrying out experiments in democratic reform at the birthplace of the student movement—the university campus, democratizing and systematizing campus life; second, to participate actively in politics, to persist in our request for a dialogue with the government, to push democratic reforms of our political system, to oppose graft and corruption, and to work for a press law. We recognize that these short-term objectives are only the first steps in democratic reform; they are tiny, unsteady steps. But we must struggle for these first steps, we must cheer for these first steps.

Fellow students, fellow countrymen, prosperity for our nation is the ultimate objective of our patriotic student movement. Democracy, science, freedom, human rights, and rule by law are the ideals that we hundreds of thousands of university students share in this struggle. Our ancient, thousand-year civilization is waiting, our great people, one billion strong, are watching. What qualms can we possibly have? What is there to fear? Fellow students, fellow countrymen, here at richly symbolic Tiananmen, let us once again search together and struggle together for democracy, for science, for freedom, for human rights, and for rule by law.

Let our cries awaken our young Republic!

*(read by Wu'er Kaixi*
*at Tiananmen Square*
*May 4, 1989)*

*Minzhu Han and Sheng Hua, eds., Cries for Democracy: Writings and Speeches from the 1989 Chinese Democracy Movement* (Princeton, NJ: Princeton University Press, 1990), 135–37.

### DISCUSSION QUESTIONS

1. How does this document link the 1989 protests to the tradition of student protest in China?
2. What is the relationship between the students and the Chinese government in May 1919? May 1989?

# Transcript of Meeting between Premier Li Peng and Students (May 18, 1989)

*The May 18 meeting between student leaders, led by Wu'er Kaixi and Wang Dan, and Premier Li Peng seemed poised to achieve the breakthroughs that*

*would become commonplace across Eastern Europe in the fall. Instead, it polar-*
*ized both sides and confirmed the worst fears of both. The students saw Li Peng*
*as unresponsive and didactic; Li felt the students were disrespectful and unwill-*
*ing to compromise. From this time forward, the hard-liners in the government—*
*already in a position of power—dominated policy toward the protesters.*

---

*[Premier] Li Peng.* I am very glad to meet you all. For today's meeting, we are going to talk about only one subject: that is, how to get the hunger strikers out of their present plight. The Party and the government are very concerned about this matter. We are also deeply disturbed by it and fear for the health of these students. Let us solve this problem first; afterward, all matters can be easily settled through discussion. We say this not out of any ulterior motives, but mainly because we are concerned. You are all very young; the oldest among you is not more than twenty-three. Even my youngest child is older than you all. I have three children and none of them is involved in profiteering by officials. But all of them are older than you. You are like our own children, our own flesh and blood.

*Wuer Kaixi.* [interrupting] Premier Li, it doesn't seem that we have enough time for this kind of talk.[1] We must enter into a substantive discussion as quickly as possible. Now, I would like to say what we have to say. Just now you have said that we were going to talk about only one subject. But the real situation is not that you invited us to this discussion, but that we, all these many people in the Square, asked you to come and talk. How many subjects to discuss, therefore, ought to be up to us. Fortunately, our views here happen to be in agreement. . . . We have heard and read Comrade Zhao Ziyang's talk that came out in writing yesterday [in which Zhao, on behalf of the Politburo, stated that the students' demands for democracy were reasonable and patriotic, and promised there would be no retaliation]. So why haven't the students gone back [to

---

[1] This translation is based on the official Xinhua News Agency transcript of the meeting. Hong Kong papers published transcripts that differed slightly from the Xinhua account and were somewhat more embarrassing to the Chinese government. Most notably, Wu'er Kaixi's opening remarks are recorded as: [interrupting Premier Li Peng] "We don't have much time. We are sitting very comfortably here, but outside the students are suffering from hunger. So excuse me very much for interrupting you. . . ."

their campuses]? Because we believe that it was still not enough, far from enough. I am sure you are aware of the conditions that we have put forth [for ending the hunger strike] as well as developments in the Square.

*Wang Dan.* Let me give a report on the situation in the Square. More than two thousand people have already lost consciousness. As for how to make them end the hunger strike and leave the Square, all the conditions we have stipulated must be fully met. . . . In this regard, our position is very clear: the only way to make the hunger strikers leave the Square is to satisfy the two demands that our students have presented to you.

*Wu'er Kaixi.* For your age, sir, I feel it might be appropriate if I call you Teacher Li. Teacher Li, the issue at this time is not at all how to persuade the group of us present here. We would very much like to have the students leave the Square. [But] right now, what's happening in the Square is not so much a case in which the minority follows the majority, but one in which 99.9 percent follow 0.1 percent—so if a single hunger striker refuses to leave the Square, then the other several thousand will not leave either.

*Wang Dan.* Yesterday, we conducted a poll among over a hundred students, asking whether or not they would agree to withdraw from the Square after our conversation with Secretary Yan Mingfu. The poll showed that 99.9 percent of the students voted against withdrawing from the Square. Here, we would like to make clear once again what our demands are: one, that the current student movement be recognized as a patriotic Democracy Movement, not a disturbance, as it has been called; and two, that a dialogue be arranged as quickly as possible and broadcast live. If the government can quickly and satisfactorily respond to these two demands, we then will be able to go and work on the students, to get them to leave the Square. Otherwise, it will be very difficult for us to do this task.

*Wu'er Kaixi.* . . . Up to the present, still no one has stated that the student movement is not turmoil. The nature of this movement must be [properly] defined. Then, we can work out several [specific] methods for [conveying this message]: (1) Comrade Zhao Ziyang or Comrade Li Peng—Zhao Ziyang would be best—could go the Square and speak directly to the students; or (2) the *People's Daily* could print another editorial repudiating the one published on April 26, one that apologizes to the people across the country and acknowledges the great significance of the current student movement. Only if this is done can we make our best efforts to persuade the students to convert the hunger strike into a sit-in protest. After we reach this point, we can proceed to solve other problems. We on our part will try our best to persuade the students, but we cannot say for sure that we will succeed.

*[Student leader] Xiong Yan:* We believe that whether or not the government or some other party acknowledges that this is a patriotic democracy movement, history will recognize it as such. But why do [we] especially need the acknowledgment of the government and the others? Because this represents a desire of the people; that is, [a desire] to see if our government is, after all, our own government. . . . Second, we are people who are struggling for the sake of communism, people of conscience, people with humanity. To resolve this kind of problem, [the government] ought not to care about "losing face," or whatever other thing. . . .

*Li Peng.* Let me raise one point. When we are talking, I hope you will be kind enough not to interrupt. When we are finished, whomever has more to say can speak again, there will be plenty of opportunities. . . .

*Yan Mingfu.* . . . The only issue that I am concerned with is that of saving the children who are hunger striking in the Square, who are now in a very weakened state, their lives gravely threatened. In my opinion, the final resolution of the issues [between us] and the issue of the hunger strike should be separated. In particular, those students who have not participated in the hunger strike must show care for the hunger strikers. I am confident that in the end we can solve all our problems. . . . We should reach an agreement that these two issues ought to be discussed separately, for the evolving situation, as I pointed out to Wuer Kaixi and Wang Dan on the evening of May 13, has already gone beyond the good intentions of those who initiated the hunger strike. They are already out of your control. . . .

*Li Peng.* Now, let me make a few points. Since you said you would like to discuss matters of substance, I will begin by discussing a matter of substance. I suggest that the China Red Cross and Beijing

Red Cross be put in charge of getting the students who are participating in the hunger strike safely to hospitals. I hope that other
students in the Square will support and assist this operation. This is
my specific proposal. In the meantime, I will ask all the medical
personnel under the jurisdiction of the Central Committee and
Beijing Municipality to do their best to rescue and take care of the
student hunger strikers, so as to ensure the absolute safety of their
lives. Regardless of how many common points of view, or disagreements, we have, saving human lives is our top priority for the moment. . . .

Second, neither the government nor the Party has ever stated
that the masses of students were creating turmoil. We have always
regarded the patriotic enthusiasm and wishes of the students as
positive and good. Many of the things you have done are quite correct; many of your criticisms correspond to what the government
sees as problems and hopes to resolve. To be frank, you have definitely provided impetus for finding solutions to these problems. . . .
Now that our students have so sharply pointed out these problems,
[their criticisms] can help the government overcome obstacles on
the road to progress. This I think is positive. However, the way the
present situation is developing does not depend on your good intentions, your idealistic visions, or patriotic enthusiasm. The fact is that
disorder has already appeared in Beijing and is spreading across the
entire country. I do not mean to pin responsibility for disorder onto
our students, absolutely not. The present state of affairs is already
objective reality. Let me tell you, my students, yesterday the Beijing-
Guangzhou railway line around the Wuhan area was blocked for
more than three hours; this caused one of our major railway transportation lines to cease operation. And right now, all sorts of idlers
and riff-raff from many cities are descending on Beijing in the
name of the students. In the past few days, Beijing has basically
fallen into a state of anarchy. Let me just reiterate, I do not mean
to pin responsibility on our students. I just hope that our students
will turn this over in their minds and think about what consequences will follow if things [are allowed to] go on like this.

The government of the People's Republic of China is one responsible to the people, and we cannot sit and watch idly. We must

protect the safety of our students, protect our factories, protect the achievements of socialism, and protect our capital. Whether or not you are willing to listen to these words, I am very glad to have had such an opportunity to tell everyone. China has experienced many episodes of turmoil. Creating turmoil was not the original intent of many people, but in the end, turmoil was what occurred.

Third, presently there are some government employees, city residents, workers, even staff from certain departments of our State Council who have taken to the streets to show their support for the students. I hope you will not misunderstand why they are doing so. It is out of their concern for you and out of the hope that you will not harm your health. However, I do not completely approve of the methods of many of these people. If they try to persuade you to eat and drink a little, in order to protect your health, if they try to persuade you to leave the Square and express whatever you have to say to the government by way of discussion, that [kind of behavior] is completely correct. But there are also many who have gone to the Square to encourage you to continue with the hunger strike. I will not say what their motives are, but I do not approve of this kind of behavior. As Premier of the government, I must make my position clear. . . .

> *[Student] Wang Zhixin.* This is not a dialogue but a meeting.
> *Yan Mingfu.* Correct, a meeting.

Minzhu Han and Sheng Hua, eds., *Cries for Democracy: Writings and Speeches from the 1989 Chinese Democracy Movement* (Princeton, NJ: Princeton University Press, 1990), 242–46.

## DISCUSSION QUESTIONS
1. What were the students' main objectives in this dialogue?
2. What were the government's main objectives in this dialogue?
3. To what do you attribute the failure of this dialogue to produce meaningful results?

# Li Peng, Speech on Behalf of Party Central Committee and State Council (May 19–20, 1989)

*Demonstrating the power of hard-liners in the government, Li Peng's address on national television confirmed that the government would use more aggressive tactics in dealing with the protests.*

[Video report, captioned: "Li Peng Delivers Important Speech on Behalf of Party Central Committee and State Council," at a meeting of cadres from party, government, and army organs of the central and Beijing municipal levels convened by the CPC Central Committee and the State Council on May 19—place not given; live or recorded [*sic*]; report is preceded by caption: "Important News"]

[Unidentified announcer] A meeting of cadres from the party, government, and army organs at the central and Beijing municipal levels was convened by the CPC Central Committee and the State Council, on the evening of May 19. On behalf of the party Central Committee and the State Council, Li Peng made an important speech.

[Video begins with a close-up of Li Peng in a Mao suit, reading from a prepared speech. During his address, video shows medium-length shots of Yang Shangkun, Qiao Shi, Hu Qili, Wang Zhen, and Yao Yilin seated, and pan shots of a conference hall with an audience of approximately 1,000 people. Video focuses on Yang Shangkun while he follows Li Peng in making a speech.]

[Li Peng] Comrades, in accordance with a decision made by the Standing Committee of the CPC Central Committee, the party Central Committee and the State Council have convened a meeting here of cadres from party, government, and army organs at the central and Beijing municipal levels, calling on everyone to mobilize in this emergency and to adopt resolute and effective measures to curb turmoil in a clear-cut manner, to restore normal order in society, and to maintain stability and unity in order to ensure the triumphant implementation of our reform and open policy and the program of socialist modernization [applause].

The briefing by Comrade Li Ximing, secretary of the Beijing Municipal Party Committee, a little while ago indicated that the current situation in the capital is quite grim. The anarchic state is going from bad to worse. Law and discipline have been undermined. Prior to the beginning of May, the situation had begun to cool down as a result of great efforts. However, the situation has become more turbulent since the beginning of May. More and more students and other people have been involved in demonstrations. Many institutions of higher learning have come to a standstill. Traffic jams have taken place everywhere. The party and government leading organs have been affected, and public security has been rapidly deteriorating. All this has seriously disturbed and undermined the normal order of production, work, study, and everyday life of the people in the whole municipality. Some activities on the agenda for state affairs of the Sino-Soviet summit that attracted worldwide attention had to be canceled, greatly damaging China's international image and prestige.

The activities of some of the students on hunger strike at Tiananmen Square have not yet been stopped completely. Their health is seriously deteriorating and some of their lives are still in imminent danger. In fact, a handful of persons are using the hunger strikers as hostages to coerce and force the party and the government to yield to their political demands. In this regard, they have not one iota of humanity [applause].

The party and the government have, on one hand, taken every possible measure, to treat and rescue the fasting students. On the other hand, they have held several dialogues with representatives of the fasting students and have earnestly promised to continue to listen to their opinions in the future, in the hope that the students would stop their hunger strike immediately. But, the dialogues did not yield results as expected. The square is packed with extremely excited crowds who keep shouting demagogic slogans. Right now, representatives of the hunger striking students say that they can no longer control the situation. If we fail to promptly put an end to such a state of affairs and let it go unchecked, it will very likely lead to serious consequences which none of us want to see.

The situation in Beijing is still developing, and has already affected many other cities in the country. In many places, the number of demonstrators and protesters is increasing. In some places, there have been many incidents of people breaking into local party and government organs, along with beating, smashing, looting, burning, and other undermining activities that seriously violated the law. Some trains running on major railway lines have even been intercepted, causing communications to stop. Something has happened to our trunk line, the Beijing-Guangzhou line. Today, a train from Fuzhou was intercepted. The train was unable to move out for several hours.

All these incidents demonstrate that we will have nationwide major turmoil if no quick action is taken to turn and stabilize the situation. Our nation's reforms and opening to the outside world, the cause of the four modernizations, and even the fate and future of the People's Republic of China, built by many revolutionary martyrs with their blood, are facing a serious threat [applause].

Our party and government have pointed out time and time again that the vast numbers of young students are kindhearted, that subjectively they do not want turmoil, and that they have fervent patriotic spirit, wishing to push forward reform, develop democracy, and overcome corruption. This is also in line with the goals which the party and government have striven to accomplish. It should be said that many of the questions and views they raise have already exerted and will continue to exert positive influence on improving the work of the party and government. However, willfully using various forms of demonstrations, boycotts of class, and even hunger strikes to make petitions have damaged social stability and will not be beneficial to solving the problems. Moreover, the situation has developed completely independent of the subjective wishes of the young students. More and more it is going in a direction that runs counter to their intentions.

At present, it has become more and more clear that the very, very few people who attempt to create turmoil want to achieve, under the conditions of turmoil, precisely their political goals which they could not achieve through normal democratic and legal channels; to negate the CPC leadership and to negate the socialist system. They openly promoted the slogan of negating the opposition to bourgeois liberalization. Their goal is to gain absolute freedom to unscrupulously oppose the four cardinal principles. They spread many rumors, attacking, slandering, and abusing principal leaders of the party and state. At present, the spearhead has been focused on Comrade Deng Xiaoping, who has made tremendous contributions to our cause of reform and opening to the outside world. Their goal is precisely to organizationally subvert the CPC leadership, overthrow the people's government elected by the People's Congress in accordance with the law, and totally negate the people's democratic dictatorship. They stir up trouble everywhere, establish secret ties, instigate the creation of all kinds of illegal organizations, and force the party, the people, and the government to recognize them. In doing so, they are attempting to lay a foundation and make a breakthrough for the establishment of opposition factions and opposition parties. If they should succeed, the reform and opening to the outside world, democracy and legality, and socialist modernization would all come to nothing, and China would suffer a historical retrogression. A very promising China with a very bright future would become a hopeless China without a future.

One important reason for us to take a clear-cut stand in opposing the turmoil and exposing the political conspiracy of a handful of people is to distinguish the masses of young students from the handful of people who incited the turmoil. For almost a month, we adopted an extremely tolerant and restrained attitude in handling the student unrest. No government in the world would be so tolerant. The reason that we were so tolerant was out of our loving care for the masses of youths and students. We regard them as our own children and the future of China. We do not want to hurt good people, particularly not the young students. However, the handful of behind-the-scenes people, who were plotting and inciting the turmoil, miscalculated and took the tolerance as weakness on the part of the party and government. They continued to cook up stories to confuse and poison the masses, in an attempt to worsen the situation. This has caused the situation in the capital and many localities across the country to become increasingly acute. Under such circumstances, the CPC, as a ruling party and a government responsible to the people, is forced to take resolute and decisive measures to put and end to the turmoil [applause].

It must be stressed that even under such circumstances, we should still persist in protecting the patriotism of the students, make a clear distinction between them and the very, very few people who created the turmoil, and not penalize students for their radical words and actions in the student movement. Moreover, dialogue will continue in an active way through various channels, in different forms, and at different levels between the party and the government on one hand and the students and people from other walks of life on the other, including dialogue with those students who have taken part in parades, demonstrations, class boycotts, and hunger strikes, in order to take full heed of opinions from all segments. We will not only give clear-cut answers to the reasonable demands raised by them, but will also pay close attention to and earnestly accept their reasonable criticisms and suggestions, such as punishing profiteering officials, getting rid of corruption, and overcoming bureaucratism as well as promoting democracy, developing education, and so forth, so as to earnestly improve the work of the party and the government.

Under extremely complicated conditions in this period, many responsible comrades and the masses of teachers and students have taken pains and done a great deal of work to try to prevent demonstrations and keep order on campuses. They have been called campus traitors for their efforts. Public security personnel and armed policemen have made great contributions in maintaining traffic, social order, and security under extremely difficult conditions. Government offices, factories, shops, enterprises, and institutions have persisted in production and work, and made strenuous efforts to keep social life in order. The party and the government are aware of all this and are grateful; the people will never forget [applause]. Now, to check the turmoil with a firm hand and quickly restore order, I urgently appeal on behalf of the party Central Committee and the State Council: First, to those students now on hunger strike at Tiananmen Square to end the fasting immediately, leave the square, receive medical treatment, and recover their health as soon as possible. Second, to the masses of students and people in all walks of life to immediately stop all parades and demonstrations, and give no more so-called support to the fasting students in the interest of humanitarianism. Whatever the intent—I will not say that their intent is ill—further support will push the fasting students to desperation [applause].

Comrades, on behalf of the party Central Committee and the State Council, I now, at this meeting, call on the whole party, the entire army, and people of all nationalities throughout the country to unite, to pull together, and to act immediately at all their posts in an effort to stop the turmoil and stabilize the situation. Party organizations at all levels must unite the broad masses, must carry out thorough and painstaking ideological and educational work, and must fully play the role of core leadership and fighting fortress in stabilizing the situation. All Communist Party members must strictly abide by party discipline. They should not only stay away from any activities harmful to stability and unity, but they should also provide an exemplary vanguard role in uniting the masses and curbing the turmoil.

Governments at various levels must enforce administrative discipline and law, conscientiously strengthen leadership and control over their regions and departments, and earnestly carry out the work of stabilizing the situation, of reform, and of economic construction.

All government functionaries must stick to their own posts and maintain normal work order. All public security personnel should make greater efforts to maintain traffic and social order, to intensify social security, and to resolutely crack down on criminal activities of all kinds that have emerged. All industrial and commercial enterprises and institutions should abide by work discipline and persist in normal production. Schools of various kinds and at various levels should maintain normal teaching order. Those on strike should resume classes unconditionally.

Comrades, our party is a party in power and our government is a people's government. To be responsible to our sacred motherland and to all people, we must adopt firm and resolute measures to end the turmoil swiftly, to maintain the leadership of the party as well as the socialist system. We believe that our actions will surely have the support of all members of the Communist Party and the Communist Youth League, as well as workers, peasants, intellectuals, democratic parties, people in various circles, and the broad masses [applause]. We believe that we will certainly have the backing of the People's Liberation Army [PLA], which is entrusted by the Constitution with guarding the country and the peaceful work of the people [applause]. At the same time, we also hope that the broad masses will fully support the PLA, the public security cadres, and the police in their efforts to maintain order in the capital [applause].

Comrades, under the conditions of resolutely safeguarding stability and unity, we must continue to adhere to the four cardinal principles, to persist in the reform and opening up to the outside world, to strengthen democracy and the legal system, to eliminate all kinds of corruption, and to strive to advance the cause of socialist modernization [applause].

[Qiao Shi] Will Comrade Shangkun please make a speech? [applause]

[Yang Shangkun] First of all, I fully support the report and the various demands that Comrade Li Peng has made on behalf of the Standing Committee of the Political Bureau. Beijing of late is actually in an anarchistic state. Basically, the work of government organs, classes in schools, transportation, industry, and so forth have all been thrown into a confused state. This confused state is, in reality, a state of anarchy. Comrade Li Peng has just said that with regard to such a historic event as the Sino-Soviet talks, we could not hold the welcoming ceremony at Tiananmen. The location was changed to the airport at the last moment. Several discussions that should have been held at the Great Hall of the People were compelled to take place at Diaoyutai Guest House. In addition, some activities previously scheduled were canceled. Such a state of affairs. . . .

[Unidentified person, interrupting] Even the wreath could not be presented.

[Yang Shangkun] Even the originally scheduled presentation of a wreath at the Monument of the People's Heroes could not be held. This has produced a very bad effect on our foreign relations. Even you had no freedom in driving here for this meeting. You had to make many detours to arrive here. You had to depart from your place one hour or more earlier in order to arrive at this meeting place in time. If this state of affairs is allowed to continue, then our capital will not be a capital. The work of the Beijing Municipality cannot be carried out, and the work of the State Council cannot be carried out. This is extremely serious.

To restore, normal order, to restore public order, to stabilize the situation in Beijing Municipality, and to restore normal order [as heard] there is no choice but to move a group of the PLA to the vicinity of Beijing [applause; pan shots show presence of several uniformed men seated in the hall, also applauding].

The military vehicles on the road which you saw just now are those of the PLA troops entering the vicinity of Beijing Municipality a short while ago. This was done out of absolute necessity. It is because the police force in Beijing Municipality has been unable to maintain order in the Municipality. In addition, nearly all the armed police and public security cadres and police in Beijing Municipality have been working hard day and night for the past month. Many comrades have been sick, yet they have had no choice but to stand on duty day and night, some without sleep for two or three days. Thus, without a group of PLA entering here to maintain public order in Beijing Municipality, order, we believe, would be very difficult to restore.

The arrival of PLA troops in the vicinity of Beijing is definitely not aimed at dealing with students. They have not come here to deal with the students. Their aim is to restore the normal order of production, of life, of work in Beijing Municipality. At the same time, they aim to protect a number of important departments and major government organs. Therefore, the stationing of the PLA troops in the capital is aimed at maintaining public security. They are, by no means, directed at the students. Everyone will be able to clearly see their activities in the next few days [applause].

That is to say that the PLA troops are compelled to enter the capital in order to restore the normal order in Beijing, maintain public security, and prevent important government organizations from being affected or stormed. I would like to explain this point clearly to all those who are present here. The PLA troops' arrival is definitely not aimed at dealing with the students. It is hoped that all trades and professions, people in various circles, and particularly people of the various democratic parties will support the PLA troops for their action to safeguard the capital and maintain public security. I hope that you will give them your full understanding and support [applause].

This is the point that I wanted to explain to you comrades here. I have nothing else to say. That is all [applause].

[Announcer] Attending the meeting were the president and vice president of the state, members of the Standing Committee of the Political Bureau of the CPC Central Committee currently in Beijing, and responsible comrades from the CPC Central

Committee, the State Council, the National People's Congress, the Central Military Commission, the Central Advisory Commission, the National Committee of the Chinese People's Political Consultative Conference, and Beijing Municipality.

At the beginning of the meeting, Li Ximing, secretary of the Beijing Municipal Party Committee, briefed the meeting about the current situation in Beijing Municipality.

Beijing Television Service, May 19–20, 1989, 15:27 Greenwich Mean Time.

## DISCUSSION QUESTIONS

1. What is the government's response based on this speech?
2. Why does it appear that the government policy toward the protests had changed?
3. What actions does Li Peng call for in the speech?

# Cui Jian, Nothing to My Name (1986)

*Cui Jian is the first rock star to emerge in the People's Republic. His music is often critical of the Chinese government, though it is usually veiled enough to avoid censorship. He appeared regularly in Tiananmen Square during the protests, and following the movement he was banned from major concerts for about ten years, and his music was informally banned from state radio stations. "Nothing to My Name" recorded in 1986, became an anthem for the protests, played on personal radios and guitars throughout the month of May, helping the students articulate their desires and fears in a changing China. The song lyrics are translated here. Cui Jian titled his next album, after 1989,* The Power of the Powerless, *evoking Václav Havel's essay of the same name.*

> I have asked you endlessly,
> When will you go with me?
> But you always laugh at me,
> [Because I have] Nothing to my name
> I want to give you my dreams,
> And give you my freedom.

But you always laugh at me,
[Because I have] Nothing to my name.
Ohhh. . . .
When will you go with me?

The earth beneath my feet is moving.
The river beside me is flowing.
But you always laugh at me,
[Because I have] Nothing to my name.
Why do you always laugh at me so?
Why don't I give up?
Why do you see me as,
Forever having nothing to my name?
Ohhh. . . .
Just go with me now!

Listen—I've waited so long,
So I'll make my final request.
I want to grab you by the hands,
And take you with me.
Now your hands are trembling,
Now your tears are falling.
Perhaps you are saying,
You love me [even though I have] nothing to my
name
Ohhh. . . .
Just go with me now.

Author's translation of song lyrics.

## DISCUSSION QUESTIONS
1. Why does this song seem an appropriate anthem for the protesters in the square?
2. Does this song's popularity with the students shed any light on
their motives or goals?

# Interview with Chai Ling (May 1989)

*In this interview with American journalist Philip Cunningham, Chai Ling—
the "commander in chief" of Tiananmen Square—appears to advocate bloodshed, sacrificing the students in order to achieve change in China. This is a
controversial interview, given in late May, because Chai Ling, by most accounts,
did not remain in Tiananmen Square when the troops arrived to clear the
Square.*

. . . The blackest day has not yet come, yet still many of our fellow
students do not understand that our presence here and now at the
Square is our last and only truth. If we withdraw, the only one to
rejoice will be the government. What goes against my inclinations
is that, as commander-in-chief, I have again and again demanded
the power to resist these capitulationists, while the Beijing Students'
Federation and the Non-Beijing Students' Federation are also anxious to have the power to make decisions. Once, at a meeting with
figures from the academic world, I felt great frustration because I
felt these people were trying to use the student movement to place
themselves in the limelight once more. I have resisted such tenden-
cies from the beginning. I have also been irritated at Wu'er Kaixi
all along; he has at times used his own influence and position in
ways that have caused great damage. Some people are now trying
to put him in the limelight again. My criticisms of him are directed
chiefly at some of the methods and angles from which he considers
things. I feel that the best days, the days of greatest unity, were
when the group of hunger-strikers was just starting out. . . .

Some fellow students asked me what our plans are, what our
demands will be in the future. This made me feel sick at heart; I
started out to tell them that what we were waiting for was actually
the spilling of blood, for only when the government descends to the
depths of depravity and decides to deal with us by slaughtering us,
only when rivers of blood flow in the Square, will the eyes of our
country's people truly be opened, and only then will they unite. But
how could I say that to my fellow students? The saddest part is that
in order to achieve their own objectives, some students—people

from higher-up levels—have asked that the government take no measures, but simply wait until our [movement] collapses. If we withdraw from the Square, that will be exactly what happens. Everyone who was not destroyed in previous political movements will be swept away with one flick of the broom. Deng Xiaoping said it correctly: there really is always a small handful, be they in the Party, in society, or among the students. If they get their way, then what will happen in China will actually be a sort of restoration of the monarchy. Forty or seventy years afterwards, there will be a great massacre, and who knows how many years it will take after that before democracy dares to stand up again. The methods they use are assassination, disappearance, and [the sowing of] spiritual dissension; these are exactly the methods they used against Wei Jingsheng. There is no way I can tell these things directly to my fellow students; it's hard for me to tell them we must awaken the masses with our blood. The students would definitely be willing to do this, but others are still just little kids! [bursts into tears] . . .

Minzhu Han and Sheng Hua, eds., *Cries for Democracy: Writings and Speeches from the 1989 Chinese Democracy Movement* (Princeton, NJ: Princeton University Press, 1990), 327–28.

## DISCUSSION QUESTIONS

1. According to this interview, how did Chai Ling intend for the occupation of Tiananmen Square to end?
2. What did Chai Ling believe this would accomplish?
3. Does this interview affect the way you interpret Chai Ling's claim that she was "commander in chief" of the Square?

# The Tank Man (June 5, 1989)

*This photograph was taken on the morning of June 5, 1989, on Chang'an Avenue, adjacent to Tiananmen Square. Shortly after the photo was taken, videotapes of the event show the man climbing atop the tank and engaging in an animated discussion with its driver, before being spirited away by onlookers and disappearing into the crowd. Although the subject of much speculation, including a documentary film titled* Tank Man, *nothing is known of his fate. Western media commentary tends to celebrate the man as a symbol of nonviolent resistance to state repression; the Chinese official media uses the same image to demonstrate the restraint of its armed forces for letting the man conduct his actions unharmed.*

CNN/Getty Images.

## DISCUSSION QUESTIONS

1. What does this image show? How do you explain what is happening?
2. Why has this image captured the imagination of the world?
3. What does the success of this image suggest about the nature of media in interpreting public protests?

# What Happened on the Night of June 3/4?
## (June 22, 1989)

*Compiling accounts from eyewitnesses, journalists, and other sources, U.S. diplomatic officials in Beijing relayed to Washington their best understanding of the events that had taken place in Tiananmen Square as the Chinese government cleared the Square and ended the protest movement; included is a detailed chronology of events.*

1. Confidential—Entire Text
2. (c) Introduction:
   According to official press reports, P.L.A. [People's Liberation Army] troops and security forces employed maximum restraint in moving into the city center, only firing when threatened by groups of violent "counter-revolutionaries." Official accounts naturally stress the violence [with] which groups of citizens attacked and/or killed soldiers.
3. (c) In the following narrative and chronology, the embassy attempts to set the record straight. Our narrative is based on eyewitness accounts of emboffs [embassy officials], western diplomats, western reporters and American students present on or near Tiananmen Square, and on credible second hand information. We conclude that, contrary to a number of early western press accounts, the massacre took place on Chang'an Ave and other of Beijing's main thoroughfares rather than in Tiananmen Square itself. Many—if not most—of the deaths occurred as the military moved toward the square from the west.
4. The P.L.A. did not fire directly on students gathered around the martyrs monument on Tiananmen square. Troops beat, and probably killed some students after they exited the square. However, other students who faced off troops in the streets around the square were shot. Many members of the crowds attempting to slow the P.L.A.'s advance threw bricks and stones at soldiers and beat and/or killed a number of them. But given the preponderance of force on the military side, it is inconceiv-

able that military casualties exceeded those on the civilian side. Civilian deaths probably did not reach the figure of 3,000 used in some press accounts, but they surely far outnumbered official figures.

5. It should be kept in mind that whatever the casualty figure, whatever the occupation of the civilians who were killed, and however violent some members of the crowd may have become, the order to move heavily armed troops on Tiananmen was cynical and inhumane.

End of Introduction.

6. (c) Precis of Events: The main military thrust that night came from the west. Large crowds engaged in pitched battles with armed troops and armored columns at intersections along Fuxing and Chang'an avenues as troops fired directly at Beijing citizens.

7. (c) Soldiers in an armored column of tanks and APCs [armored personnel carriers] that entered Tiananmen from the east after [illegible] June 4 also fired indiscriminately at crowds along the route. Battles between troops and citizens also apparently took place south of Tiananmen Square, probably at the Chongwenmen intersections and along Qianmen Avenue. We have also heard of heavy fighting [illegible] just south of Qianmen. We have no western eyewitness accounts of the events at Chongwenman, Qianmen Avenue, and Dazhalan, however.

8. (c) Casualties also occurred in the Tiananmen area after troops and armor arrived at the north end of the square sometime between 0130 and 0200, June 4. Here, crowds on Chang'an Avenue on the Northeast side of the square faced off troops who had entered from the northwest. Troops fired directly at this crowd throughout the morning between Tiananmen Square and the Beijing Hotel.

9. (c) The battles raged around the square rather than on it. Witnesses present at the martyrs' monument described an eerie lack of action on the square proper during the shooting in the streets. We have heard no accounts of soldiers firing directly at

students crowded around the martyrs' monument on the square. Eyewitnesses also state that, as far as they could tell, no students were present in the tents which APCs rolled over as they entered the square proper before sunrise on June 4. The several thousand students who remained at the monument departed the square via the southeast corner beginning at about 0500 [5 A.M.], June 4.

10. (c) Eyewitness accounts of what happened to the students once they left are few. Western Journalists who were present or who heard from eyewitnesses agree that students departed via the southeast corner of the square onto Qianmen Avenue. They were split into groups, some of which travelled east, some west.

11. (c) Journalists present on the square at this time state that police or P.L.A. troops in riot gear beat some of the departing students. An eyewitness told an American journalist that tanks moving west on Chang'an Avenue ran over and killed ten students who marched west from the square and then north to the vicinity of the Beijing concert hall. The eyewitness told the journalist that soldiers shot and killed at least one of the students accompanying those who were run over by the tanks.

12. (c) Casualties: We may never know precisely how many troops and civilians died or were injured on the night of June 3/4 and in following days. The true figure is probably over one thousand; not over one hundred as the Chinese officials claim. Soon after the massacre, the Kyodo news service reported that the Chinese red cross gave a figure of 2,000 military and civilian deaths with 7,000 on both sides, wounded, based on a canvass of Beijing hospitals. (Note: These deaths were recorded in hospitals and reportedly do not include deaths on the street. End note.) Beijing-based Japanese diplomats find the Kyodo source credible and the estimate convincing.
Our [illegible] believes that this is not an unreasonable estimate, given the nature of the conflict and the weapons used by the P.L.A.

13. (c) Official casualty statistics differ markedly from this, but they are contradictory. At a June 7 press conference, state council spokesman Yuan Mu stated that total deaths of troops and civilians numbered "around 300 people." According to Yuan

"over 5,000 troops" suffered injuries, with "over 3,000" civilians injured. However, a June 14 Xinhua release reported that "nearly 100 soldiers and policemen and thousands of soldiers and policemen were wounded." "Some 100 civilians were killed and nearly 3,000 were injured," according to Xinhua.

14. Beijing Hospitals have been unwilling to discuss casualty figures. Emboffs visiting three hospitals on the afternoon of June 4 witnessed or were told of a total of [illegible] civilians dead at these three hospitals alone. Among the dead were women and at least one child. A western journalist who visited seven hospitals between June 4 and June 7, including those visited by Emboffs, was told of 156 civilian deaths at these hospitals. These figures are necessarily low, given our inability to visit hospitals systematically.

15. (c) Student deaths as this June 7 press conference, Yuan Mu claimed that as of that day, only 23 Beijing students had died as a result of the military movement on the city's center. He said that this figure resulted from investigations at local universities. Western journalists who have visited major Beijing campuses have found that student sources can confirm by name the deaths of only 3–18 at each of several major universities, but a western academic was told by professors that a larger number of students are still unaccounted for (e.g., 17 each at Beijing and Qinghua universities). The state council has released no figures on the deaths of students who are from universities outside the capital. The non-Beijing students formed the majority of student demonstrators in the square itself by June 3.

16. (c) Below is a chronology of the events of the night of June 3/4. Begin Chronology:

## June 3

1500   Large crowds of Beijing citizens around Tiananmen Square; several thousand unarmed P.L.A. troops hemmed in by crowds at west gate of great hall of the people (GHOP).

1600   Violence flares at [illegible] (south entrance to Zhongnanhai) as troops guarding gate fire into air and beat some demonstrators with belts.

1800    P.L.A. troops fire on crowd surrounding troop trucks at Muxidi and Fuxingmen; number of casualties unknown.

2000    Crowds encircle convoy of 20–30 trucks bearing armed troops at Jianguomen and third ring road, this scene repeated on major intersections surrounding city.

2030    Troops at West Gate of GHOP retreat inside.

2200    Troops on truck at Yanjing Hotel, between Muxidi and Fuxingmen fire on crowd in street, casualties unknown.

2300    Armed P.L.A. troops in truck surround by crowds in front of Beijing Hotel.

## June 4

0030    Bus blockade at Fuxingmen burns. P.L.A. fires on crowds. Column of APCs approaches Fuxingmen. At least 30 casualties reported at this site.

Police or troops in riot gear with shields engage in pitched battle with crowd of over 10,000 people in front of Minzu hotel; crowd composed of people of all ages and sexes; they jeer at riot police, some throw bricks and stones, riot police responded with small arms fire above crowd and tear gas.

Crowd disperses as infantry line avenue to secure lane for approaching APCs; members of crowd still lining the avenue throw rocks and fire bombs. Infantry responds with direct fire; casualties witnessed, but numbers unknown.

0000–0030    First two APCs enter vicinity of Tiananmen Square.

0100    Demonstrators set afire one APC North of the square on Chang'an Avenue; First official warnings to leave square broadcast over Tiananmen PA [public address] system; column of APCs from West passes Zhongnanhai.

0150    Infantry heading for square passes North gate of GHOP, fires directly on large crowd gathered on Chang'an. Avenue North of square; crowd retreats east, many casualties reported, but numbers unknown.

0200    Majority of students remaining at square gather at the base of martyrs monument, Emboff estimates their number at 5,000; Reliable western diplomat witnesses "many" demonstrators with severe head and chest wounds carried off Chang'an avenue.

0210   "Suicide bus" heads West on Chang'an for approaching armor column.

0300   Students request negotiations with P.L.A.; armed infantry enters the square from southeast to enter GHOP; they are jeered by crowds.

0330   Students vote to leave square.

0400   Several thousand armed P.L.A. troops appear on east steps of GHOP, the[ir] bayonets fixed; P.L.A. or People's Armed Police units also appear on steps of history museum armed with truncheons.

Lights out on Tiananmen Square.

0430–0445   APCs that entered from the West now lined up at the Gate of Heavenly Peace facing south; they begin to move into the square proper, running over student tents.

Sound of heavy fire reported from southeast of square; could have come from Chongwenmen area, where heavy fighting and many casualties were later reported.

0420   Lights on in square.

0430   Troops or Police in riot gear appear within grounds of Mao Mausoleum south of monument.

0500–0530   Students begin to leave monument for southeast end of square and exit from there onto Qianmen Avenue; some move east, others west.

0500   Tanks enter Tiananmen Square from south.

0510   "Goddess of Liberty" statue is down.

0545   Armored column of [illegible] tanks, 25 APC's and many troop trucks enters Tiananmen from the east; Elements of this column fire heavily and indiscriminately at crowds gathered along Chang'an Avenue.

0600   Last students depart square, some beaten by troops in riot gear.

0620   Another armed column enters Tiananmen from the east; its troops also fire indiscriminately at crowds.

0650   Approximately 35 tanks enter square.

1025–1210   Four separate incidents of indiscriminate fire on crowds in front of Beijing Hotel; at least 50 civilian casualties.

End of Chronology.

Note: Sporadic killing continued at least through Wednesday, June 6. We have heard numerous first- and second-hand reports of soldiers firing on groups of students and other citizens who expressed opposition to the crackdown. Lilley.

National Security Archive at George Washington University; available at http://www.gwu.edu/~nsarchiv.

## DISCUSSION QUESTIONS

1. According to this report, how many casualties (protesters, other civilians, and military) were likely during the clearing of the Square? When, where, and how were most of these casualties incurred?
2. How does this description of events compare with official versions from Chinese government sources, or with those of student activists or survivors?
3. How can we assess the reliability of this report?

## Africa

# The Mandela Document (July 5, 1989)

*In July 1989, South African persident P. W. Botha arranged an unprecedented meeting with political prisoner Nelson Mandela. Botha had suffered a stroke earlier in the year and had already announced his retirement for September. Before the meeting, Mandela presented Botha with the so-called Mandela Document, which outlined many of his views as well as the positions of his organization, the African National Congress or ANC. While Mandela began his career as a follower of Gandhi and an advocate of nonviolence, he adopted guerrilla tactics in the early 1960s, when no end to the racial apartheid system was in sight. He was imprisoned in 1963 and became an international symbol of racial repression in South Africa. In this document, excerpted here, Mandela clarified his views on violence as well as his position on Marxism and socialism. The national government of South Africa often justified its racial laws as preventing the spread of communism during the Cold War.*

The deepening political crisis in our country has been a matter of grave concern to me for quite some time and I now consider it necessary in the national interest for the African National Congress and the government to meet urgently to negotiate an effective political settlement.

At the outset I must point out that I make this move without consultation with the ANC. I am a loyal and disciplined member of the ANC, my political loyalty is owed, primarily, if not exclusively, to this organisation and particularly to our Lusaka headquarters where the official leadership is stationed and from where our affairs are directed.

[ * * * ]

## My Release Not the Issue

I must further point out that the question of my release from prison is not an issue, at least at this stage of the discussions, and I am certainly not asking to be freed. But I do hope that the government will, as soon as possible, give me the opportunity from my present quarters to sound the views of my colleagues inside and outside the country on this move. Only if this initiative is formally endorsed by the ANC will it have any significance.

[ * * * ]

## Current Views among Blacks

I must add that the purpose of this discussion is not only to urge the government to talk to the ANC, but it is also to acquaint you with the views current among blacks, especially those in the Mass Democratic Movement.

If I am unable to express these views frankly and freely, you will never know how the majority of South Africans think on the policy and actions of the government; you will never know how to deal with their grievances and demands. It is perhaps proper to remind you that the media here and abroad has given certain public figures in this country a rather negative image not only in regard to human rights questions, but also in respect to their prescriptive stance when dealing with black leaders generally.

The impression is shared not only by the vast majority of blacks but also by a substantial section of the whites. If I had allowed myself to be influenced by this impression, I would not even have thought of making this move. Nevertheless, I have come here with and open mind and the impression I will carry away from this meeting will be determined almost exclusively by the manner in which you respond to my proposal.

It is in this spirit that I have undertaken this mission, and I sincerely hope that nothing will be done or said here that will force me to revise my views on this aspect.

[* * *]


## Renunciation of Violence

The position of the ANC on the question of violence is very simple. The organisation has no vested interest in violence. It abhors any action which may cause loss of life, destruction of property and misery to the people. It has worked long and patiently for a South Africa of common values and for an undivided and peaceful non-racial state. But we consider the armed struggle a legitimate form of self-defence against a morally repugnant system of government which will not allow even peaceful forms of protest.

It is more than ironical that it should be the government which demands that we should renounce violence. The government knows only too well that there is not a single political organisation in this country, inside and outside parliament, which can ever compare with the ANC in its total commitment to peaceful change.

Right from the early days of its history, the organisation diligently sought peaceful solutions and, to that extent, it talked patiently to successive South African governments, a policy we tried to follow in dealing with the present government.


## Apartheid Violence

Not only did the government ignore our demands for a meeting, instead it took advantage of our commitment to a non-violent struggle and unleashed the most violent form of racial oppression this country has ever seen. It stripped us of all basic human rights, outlawed our organisations and barred all channels of peaceful resistance. It met our demands with force and, despite the grave problems facing the country, it continues to refuse to talk to us. There can only be one answer to this challenge; violent forms of struggle.

Down the years oppressed people have fought for their birthright by peaceful means, where that was possible, and through force where peaceful channels were closed. The history of this country also confirms this vital lesson. Africans as well as Afrikaners were, at one time or other, compelled to take up arms in defence of their freedom against British imperialism. The fact that both were finally defeated by superior arms, and by the vast resources of that empire, does not negate this lesson.

But from what has happened in South Africa during the last 40 years, we must conclude that now that the roles are reversed, and the Afrikaner is no longer a freedom fighter, but is in power, the entire lesson of history must be brushed aside. Not even a disciplined non-violent protest will now be tolerated. To the government a black man has neither a just cause to espouse nor freedom rights to defend. The whites must have the monopoly of political power, and of committing violence against innocent and defenceless people. That situation was totally unacceptable to us and the formation of Umkhonto we Sizwe was intended to end that monopoly, and to forcibly bring home to the government that the oppressed people of this country were prepared to stand up and defend themselves.

It is significant to note that throughout the past four decades, and more especially over the last 26 years, the government has met our demands with force only and has done hardly anything to create a suitable climate for dialogue. On the contrary, the government continues to govern with a heavy hand, and to incite whites against negotiation with the ANC. The publication of the booklet Talking with the ANC . . . which completely distorts the history and policy of the ANC, the extremely offensive language used by government spokesmen against freedom fighters, and the intimidation of whites who want to hear the views of the ANC at first hand, are all part of the government's strategy to wreck meaningful dialogue.

Available at http://www.africawithin.com/mandela/mandela_document.htm.

## DISCUSSION QUESTIONS

1. What goals does Nelson Mandela present for his party's response to the political crisis in South Africa?
2. How do these goals compare to those of the protesters in Eastern Europe and China?
3. What do you perceive to be the relationship among the movements in all three places?

# Part IV
## Aftermath

**China**

## Deng Xiaoping, Remarks to Martial Law Officers (June 9, 1989)

*A few days after the demonstrations were crushed, Deng Xiaoping's address to soldiers who were enforcing martial law gave the government's official verdict of the demonstrations, their origins, and their suppression. The speech does not only address the actions of May and June 1989, but also fits them into the larger context of China's post-Mao reforms and development.*

Comrades, you have been working hard! . . .

This disturbance was bound to come sooner or later. It was determined by the international macro climate and China's micro climate. It was definitely coming and was something that could not be diverted by man's will; it was only a matter of time and scale. For it to occur now is advantageous for us. The biggest advantage for us is that we have a large group of old comrades who are still living and healthy. They have gone through many disturbances; they understand the complexities and subtleties of matters. They supported taking firm steps against the upheaval. Although there were some comrades who for some time did not understand, in the end they will understand, and they will support this decision of the Central Committee.

The April 26 *People's Daily* editorial defined the nature of the problem as "turmoil." This word "turmoil" exactly describes the problem. What some people opposed was this word; what they demanded revised was this word. [But] as our experience has proven, the judgment was correct. Subsequently, the situation developed into a counter-revolutionary rebellion; this was also inevitable. . . . It was relatively easy for us to handle the present explosion. The main difficulty in handling the matter is that we have never before encountered this kind of situation in which a small handful of bad persons were mixed into the masses of so many young students and onlookers. For a while, we could not distinguish the good from the bad; this made it difficult to take many steps that we should have taken. If there had not been so many elder comrades in the Party who gave us their support, then even grasping the nature of the matter would have been difficult. Some comrades do not understand the nature of the problem and believed that it was purely a problem of how to deal with the masses. In reality, the opposing side is not only a mass of people who exchange truth for lies. It is also consists of a group of people who have created an opposition faction, and many dregs of society. They want to subvert our country and subvert our Party: this is the [true] nature of the problem. . . .

Was the general conclusion of the Thirteenth Party Congress of "One Center, Two Fundamental Points" correct? Are the "Two Fundamental Points"—namely, supporting the Four Cardinal Principles and continuing the policy to reform and opening up to the outside—wrong? Recently, I have been pondering this question. We are not wrong. Adhering to the Four Cardinal Principles [adherence to socialism, adherence to the "people's democratic dictatorship," leadership of the Chinese Communist Party, and adherence to Marxism, Leninism, and Maoism] was not in itself a mistake; if there has been any error, it has been our not adequately implementing them. We have failed to make the Four Cardinal Principles the basic framework for educating people, students, and all officials and Party members. The nature of this incident is the antagonism between bourgeois liberalism and adherence to the Four Cardinal Principles. . . .

Was the basic policy of reform and opening up a mistake? No. Had there not been reform and opening up, how could we be where we are today? In the last ten years, there has been a relatively big improvement in the living standards of the people. It should be said that we have climbed up a step; even though inflation and other problems have appeared, the accomplishments of the last ten years of reform and opening up are more than enough. Of course, the policy inevitably brings with it many [negative] Western influences; we have never underestimated this [danger]. . . .

Our basic approaches, from [overall] strategies down to [specific] policies, including the policy of reform and opening up, are all correct. If there is anything that has been insufficient, it is that there is still not enough reform and opening up. We will encounter more challenging problems in the course of reform than in the course of opening up. In the reform of the political system, there is one point that can be affirmed: we will adhere to implementing the system of the National People's Congress rather than the American-style system of the separation of three powers. In reality, Western nations also do not carry out a system of separation of powers. The U.S. condemns us for suppressing the students. But when they handle domestic riots and student demonstrations, don't they send in the police and the army? Aren't there arrests and bloodshed? They suppress students and people; on the contrary, we are putting down a counter-revolutionary rebellion. What credentials do they have for judging us?! From today on, when we handle this kind of problem, we must pay attention to see that when unrest appears, we cannot allow it to spread.

---

Minzhu Han and Sheng Hua, eds., *Cries for Democracy: Writings and Speeches from the 1989 Chinese Democracy Movement* (Princeton, NJ: Princeton University Press, 1990), 368–70.

## DISCUSSION QUESTIONS
1. Why did Deng Xiaoping see the protests as "inevitable"?
2. Does Deng see the protests as indicating that mistakes were made during the reform process?
3. What does Deng advocate as proper policy toward dissent going forward?

# Introduction, *The Truth about The Beijing Turmoil* (1990)

*In 1990, the Chinese government published an album of photographs presenting its version of the events of spring 1989. This book was widely available at tourist sites and bookstores throughout China. The photos focused, often in gory detail, on atrocities and mistreatment directed toward police officers and soldiers. The introduction reproduced here summarizes the official government opinion on the demonstration and its suppression.*

In 1989 when spring was passing to summer, a shocking turmoil happened in Beijing, which has attracted the close attention of people at home and abroad. Influenced by foreign media, people have many questions, guesses and misunderstandings. What really happened in China? What is the situation now like in Beijing? This album, with its abundant pictures, will help our readers understand the whole story of and truth about the turmoil and the present situation in Beijing.

This turmoil was not a chance occurrence. It was a political turmoil incited by a very small number of political careerists after a few years of plotting and scheming. It was aimed at subverting the socialist People's Republic. By making use of some failings in the work of the Chinese government and the temporary economic difficulties, they spread far and wide many views against the Constitution, the leadership of the Chinese Communist Party and the People's Government, preparing the ground for the turmoil ideologically, organizationally and in public opinion. The former general secretary of the Central Committee of the Chinese Communist Party Zhao Ziyang supported the turmoil and thus has unshirkable responsibility for its formation and development. The various political forces and reactionary organizations abroad had a hand in the turmoil from the very beginning. Some newspapers, magazines and broadcasting stations, especially the Voice of America, fabricated rumours to mislead people, thus adding fuel to the flames.

When Hu Yaobang suddenly died on April 15, a handful of people, thinking that their time had come, stirred up a student upheaval on the pretext of "mourning" for Hu Yaobang. The student unrest had been taken advantage of by the organizers of the turmoil from the very beginning. In violation of the Constitution, laws and regulations, some people put up big-character posters everywhere on the college campuses, preaching bourgeois liberalization and calling for the overthrow of the Communist Party and the legal government. They held many rallies, made speeches, boycotted classes and organized demonstrations, all without permission; they stormed the seat of the Party Central Committee and the State Council; they forcibly occupied the Tiananmen Square on many occasions and organized various illegal organizations without registration for approval. In Changsha, Xi'an and other cities, some people engaged in grave criminal activities such as beating, smashing, looting and burning stores, and even broke into the compounds of provincial government seats and set fire to the motor vehicles there.

In view of this turmoil, the *People's Daily* issued, on April 26, an editorial exposing the nature of the turmoil. Even under this circumstance, the Party and the government exercised great restraint towards the students' extremist slogans and actions and had all along given due recognition to the students' patriotic enthusiasm and reasonable demands. At the same time, the Party and the government warned the students not to be made use of by a handful of people and expressed the hope for solving the problems through dialogues and by normal, democratic and legal procedures. However, on May 13, the illegal student organization started a general hunger strike involving over 3,000 people and lasting for seven days. Party and government leaders, on the one hand, went to see the fasting students at Tiananmen Square and met with students' representatives on many occasions, asking them to value their lives and stop the hunger strike, and on the other hand, they lost no time in organizing on-the-spot rescue teams and providing all kinds of materials so as to relieve the suffering of the fasting students. Thanks to efforts of the government and other quarters, not a single student died in the hunger strike. But all this failed to win active response. On the contrary, some media, taking the cue from a small number of people, wrongly guided the public opinion, escalating the turmoil and throwing Beijing and even the whole country in a serious anarchic situation, something that cannot be tolerated in any other country. In Beijing, demonstrations were held continuously, slogans insulting and attacking leaders and openly calling for overthrowing the government could be heard and seen everywhere. The traffic was seriously congested and difficulties were created for Beijing's production and daily supplies. The police was unable to keep normal social order. Gorbachev's schedules in China were also seriously hampered. The small handful of people attempted to take the chaos as an opportunity to seize political power and threatened to "set up a new government in three days."

On May 19, the Party Central Committee held a meeting attended by cadres from the Party, government and military institutions in Beijing. At the meeting, Premier Li Peng and President of the People's Republic of China Yang Shangkun announced the decision to adopt resolute measures to stop the turmoil. But Zhao Ziyang, then general secretary of the Party Central Committee, refused to attend this important meeting.

On May 20, Li Peng signed a martial law order as empowered by Clause 16 of Article 89 of the Constitution of the People's Republic of China. The martial law was to be enforced at 10 a.m. on the same day in parts of Beijing. The small handful of people took fright and coerced those residents who were in the dark about the truth to set up roadblocks at major crossroads to stop the advance of army vehicles and prevent the martial law enforcement troops from getting to designated places according to plan. Besides, they threatened to mobilize 200,000 people to occupy Tiananmen Square and organize a nation-wide general strike. Using the funds provided by reactionary forces at home and abroad, they installed sophisticated communication facilities and illegally purchased weapons. They gathered together hooligans and ruffians to set up terrorist organizations such as the "Dare-to-Die Corps" and the "Flying Tiger Team," and threatened to kidnap or put Party and government leaders under house arrest. They offered high prices in recruiting thugs and fabricated rumours to deceive people.

All the facts proved that, no matter how tolerant and restrained the government was, such people would not give up their wild scheme; on the contrary they threatened to "fight to the end" against the government.

On the evening of June 2, a handful of people bent upon inciting a riot used a traffic accident to spread rumours and mislead
people, lighting the fuse of a rebellion. In the small hours of June
3, rioters set up roadblocks at every crossroad, beat up soldiers and
armed police, seized weapons, ammunition and other military materials. Mobs also assaulted the Great Hall of the People, the
Central Propaganda Department, the Ministry of Public Security,
the Ministry of Radio, Film and Television and the west and south
gates of Zhongnanhai, the seat of the Party Central Committee
and the State Council. At about 5 p.m., the illegal organizations
distributed kitchen knives, daggers and iron bars, to the crowd on
Tiananmen Square and incited them to "take up weapons and
overthrow the government." A group of ruffians banded together
about 1,000 people to push down the wall of a construction site
near Xidan and seized large quantities of tools, reinforcing bars
and bricks, ready for street fighting. They planned to incite people
to take to the streets the next day, a Sunday, to stage a violent rebellion in an attempt to overthrow the government and seize power at
one stroke.

At this critical juncture, the martial law troops were ordered to
move in by force to quell the anti-government rebellion. At 6:30
p.m., on June 3, the Beijing municipal government and the headquarters of the martial law enforcement troops issued an emergency announcement, asking all citizens to keep off the streets and
stay at home. The announcement was broadcast over and over
again. At about 10 p.m., the martial law troops headed for Beijing
proper from various directions. The rioters, taking advantage of
the soldiers' restraint, blocked military and other kinds of vehicles
before they smashed and burned them. They also seized guns, am-
munitions and transceivers. Several rioters seized an armoured car
and fired guns as they drove it along the street. Rioters also assaulted civilian installations and public buildings. Several rioters
even drove a public bus loaded with gasoline drums towards the
Tiananmen gatetower in an attempt to set fire to it. At the same
time, rioters savagely beat up, kidnapped and killed soldiers and
officers. On the Chang'an Avenue, when a military vehicle suddenly broke down, rioters surrounded it and ferociously crushed
the driver with bricks. At Fuchengmen, a soldier's body was hung

heel over head on the overpass balustrade after he had been savagely killed. At Chongwenmen, another soldier was thrown down from the flyover and burned alive. Near a cinema, an officer was beaten to death, disembowelled and his eyes gouged out. His body was then strung up on a burning bus.

Over 1,280 vehicles were burned or damaged in the rebellion, including over 1,000 military trucks, more than 60 armoured cars, over 30 police cars, over 120 public buses and trolley buses and over 70 motor vehicles of other kinds. More than 6,000 martial law officers and soldiers were injured and scores of them killed.

Such heavy losses are eloquent testimony to the restraint and tolerance shown by the martial law enforcement troops. For fear of injuring civilians by accident, they would rather endure humiliation and meet their death unflinchingly, although they had weapons in their hands. It can be said that there is no other army in the world that can exercise restraint to such an extent.

The martial law troops, having suffered heavy casualties and been driven beyond forbearance, were forced to fire into the air to clear the way forward. During the counter-attack, some rioters were killed, some onlookers were hit by stray bullets and some wounded or killed by armed ruffians. According to reliable statistics, more than 3,000 civilians were wounded and over 200, including 36 college students, were killed.

At 1:30 a.m. on June 4, the Beijing municipal government and the martial law headquarters issued an emergency notice asking all students and other citizens to leave Tiananmen Square. The notice was broadcast repeatedly for well over three hours over loudspeakers. The students on Tiananmen Square, after discussion among themselves, sent representatives to the troops to express their willingness to withdraw from the square and this was approved by the troops. Then at about 5 a.m., several thousand students left the square in an orderly manner through a wide corridor in the southeastern part of the square vacated by the troops, carrying their own banners and streamers. Those who refused to leave were forced to leave by the soldiers. By 5:30 a.m., the clearing operation of the square had been completed.

During the whole operation not a single person was killed. The allegations that "Tiananmen Square was plunged into a bloodbath" and "thousands of people were killed in the square" are sheer rumours, and the true state of affairs will eventually be clear to the public.

After the decisive victory in quelling the riot, order in the capital was basically restored to normal and the situation throughout China soon became stable. The measures adopted by the Chinese government to stop the turmoil and put down the rebellion have not only won the acclaim and support of the Chinese people, but they have also won the understanding and support of the governments and people of many other countries. The Chinese government has announced that it will unswervingly carry on the policy of reform and opening to the outside world, the policy of developing friendly cooperation with different countries of the world on the basis of the five principles of peaceful coexistence, and the policy towards Hong Kong, Macao and Taiwan. We will continue to strive for the realization of the socialist modernization. We are fully confident of our future.

---

*The Truth about the Beijing Turmoil,* edited by the Editorial Board of the Truth about the Beijing Turmoil (Beijing: Beijing Publishing House, 1990), 3–5.

## DISCUSSION QUESTIONS
1. How does the Chinese government account for the unrest in Beijing in 1989?
2. What fears and goals does this document suggest are motivating the Chinese government in the aftermath of the Beijing Spring?

# Wu'er Kaixi, As Survivors, Our Lives No Longer Belong to Us Alone (June 28, 1989)

---

*Wu'er Kaixi, an ethnic Uighur from Xinjiang Province in China's far West, was a student at Beijing Normal University in 1989. He became one of the public faces of the student movement, especially for his participation in the hunger strike and for his aggressive questioning of Chinese Premier Li Peng during student-government dialogue on May 18. In the days and weeks after the clearing of the square, many survivors of the protest escaped China, while others were captured and imprisoned by the government. This document shows Wu'er Kaixi's commitment to pursuing democratic change in the face of government repression, which he has continued as a politician and radio host in Taiwan.*

I speak to all you compatriots who hold freedom and democracy dear, to the entire Chinese people. I am Wuer Kaixi of Beijing Normal University, a representative of the Beijing Students' Federation and of the Beijing student movement. I am also one of the twenty-one "counter-revolutionary rebels" on the so-called "wanted" list circulated by the pretender government. . . .

I would like to state simply that on June 4, one of the blackest days in the history of the People's Republic, our motherland became sick. In the early hours of the morning of that day, the reactionary warlords, reactionary government, and fascist military, directed and headed by Li Peng and Yang Shangkun, and controlled from behind the scenes by Deng Xiaoping, revealed themselves as the cruelly bestial fascists they are by firing upon tens of thousands of students who had gathered peacefully to petition for the redress of grievances. I must tell you that although I naturally cannot at this time give precise figures for the number of dead and wounded, still I may tell you that that night at Tiananmen Square there were at least several thousand people killed. . . .

Our fervent hope was for peace; how innocent we were! The fascists' violence was completely beyond our conception. When we started out we never so much as imagined that these beasts would descend to such depths! . . .

The presence of our fellow students will linger forever on Chang'an Avenue and Tiananmen Square. How many souls there must be howling with anger all along Chang'an Avenue! May they rest in peace!

As survivors, our lives no longer belong to us alone: our lives now include those of our fellow students and compatriots who gave their lives for democracy, for freedom, for our beautiful motherland, and for her strength and prosperity. Their lives have been melded together with ours. . . .

I believe that the memory of these martyrs will live forever. They are like the laborers on the towpaths [of the Yangtze Gorges]: they gave their lifeblood in an effort to keep the sinking ship of China away from dangerous shoals and lead her toward the bright and open ocean.

Compatriots! Comrades! Warriors of patriotism and democracy! I am Wu'er Kaixi, and I wish to say that although the great massacre is past, and events in China are temporarily at a low ebb, I still believe that our movement will be victorious in the end. Our demands must be realized in the motherland; we will most certainly launch another much larger movement for democracy and completely overthrow the reactionary warlords. . . . On this basis, we must ensure that every Chinese person has democratic consciousness. What is democracy? Many people have asked me this. Democracy means that the people control governmental power, and not the other way around. It means that people are free to choose a political-economic system that accords with their own wishes. This is democracy; it means implanting a glorious democratic consciousness into the mind of every citizen of the People's Republic of China. In the past we have failed to do this; our education has been very poor. The level achieved by our children has been very low, and the average level among our citizens is very low. Our true task is to raise the quality of our citizenry! . . .

Our purpose is not simply the overthrow of Li Peng. Whether we overthrow him or not is unimportant; but whether or not we can shout, "Down with Li Peng!" is very important. What we want is not simply the overthrow of the man, but the establishment of governmental checks and balances in China, so that we have real democratic institutions in China. I think that all of us, including our patriotic compatriots overseas, have the duty and the responsibility to join themselves with grass-roots political forces that can constitute such checks and balances, to join with these forces that can speak for the people. This is our ultimate goal! At present our task is to break the news blackout and cultivate democratic consciousness among the Chinese people; our long-range task is to build grass-roots political forces that will serve as the basis for governmental checks and balances.

Excerpt from videotape broadcast in Hong Kong, June 28, 1989. In Minzhu Han and Sheng Hua, eds., *Cries for Democracy: Writings and Speeches from the 1989 Chinese Democracy Movement* (Princeton, NJ: Princeton University Press, 1990), 376–77.

## DISCUSSION QUESTIONS

1. What does Wu'er Kaixi see as the main causes of the failure of the democracy movement in China?
2. What are his hopes and expectations for the movement's future?
3. Do subsequent events bear out his opinions? Why do you think his predictions may have varied from what actually took place?

# Fourteenth Dalai Lama, Nobel Peace Prize Acceptance Speech (December 10, 1989)

*The fourteenth Dalai Lama has lived in exile from China since 1957. As the spiritual leader of Tibetans, he has worked for greater autonomy for Tibet within China. His selection as a Nobel laureate was a clear challenge to the Chinese government—which regards the Dalai Lama as criminal "splittist." In his acceptance speech, His Holiness draws parallels between the suppression of the 1989 student protests and the continuing persecution of Tibetans. In so doing, he shows that 1989 did not resolve issues that had been ongoing throughout the twentieth century and foreshadows the continuing struggles for Tibetans and others in China.*

Your Majesty, Members of the Nobel Committee, Brothers and Sisters:

I am very happy to be here with you today to receive the Nobel Prize for Peace. I feel honoured, humbled and deeply moved that you should give this important prize to a simple monk from Tibet. I am no one special. But, I believe the prize is a recognition of the true values of altruism, love, compassion and nonviolence which I try to practise, in accordance with the teachings of the Buddha and the great sages of India and Tibet.

I accept the prize with profound gratitude on behalf of the oppressed everywhere and for all those who struggle for freedom and work for world peace. I accept it as a tribute to the man who founded the modern tradition of nonviolent action for change— Mahatma Gandhi—whose life taught and inspired me. And, of course, I accept it on behalf of the six million Tibetan people, my brave countrymen and women inside Tibet, who have suffered and continue to suffer so much. They confront a calculated and systematic strategy aimed at the destruction of their national and cultural identities. The prize reaffirms our conviction that with truth, courage and determination as our weapons, Tibet will be liberated.

No matter what part of the world we come from, we are all basically the same human beings. We all seek happiness and try to avoid suffering. We have the same basic human needs and concerns. All of us human beings want freedom and the right to determine our own destiny as individuals and as peoples. That is human nature. The great changes that are taking place everywhere in the world, from Eastern Europe to Africa, are a clear indication of this.

In China the popular movement for democracy was crushed by brutal force in June this year. But I do not believe the demonstrations were in vain, because the spirit of freedom was rekindled among the Chinese people and China cannot escape the impact of this spirit of freedom sweeping many parts of the world. The brave students and their supporters showed the Chinese leadership and the world the human face of that great nation.

Last week a number of Tibetans were once again sentenced to prison terms of up to nineteen years at a mass show trial, possibly intended to frighten the population before today's event. Their only "crime" was the expression of the widespread desire of Tibetans for the restoration of their beloved country's independence.

The suffering of our people during the past forty years of occupation is well documented. Ours has been a long struggle. We know our cause is just. Because violence can only breed more violence and suffering, our struggle must remain nonviolent and free of hatred. We are trying to end the suffering of our people, not to inflict suffering upon others.

It is with this in mind that I proposed negotiations between Tibet and China on numerous occasions. In 1987, I made specific proposals in a five-point plan for the restoration of peace and human rights in Tibet. This included the conversion of the entire Tibetan plateau into a Zone of Ahimsa, a sanctuary of peace and nonviolence where human beings and nature can live in peace and harmony.

Last year, I elaborated on that plan in Strasbourg, at the European Parliament. I believe the ideas I expressed on those occasions are both realistic and reasonable, although they have been criticised by some of my people as being too conciliatory. Unfortunately, China's leaders have not responded positively to the suggestions we have made, which included important concessions. If this continues we will be compelled to reconsider our position. Any relationship between Tibet and China will have to be based on the principle of equality, respect, trust and mutual benefit. It will also have to be based on the principle which the wise rulers of Tibet and China laid down in a treaty as early as 823 A.D., carved on the pillar which still stands today in front of the Jo-khang, Tibet's holiest shrine, in Lhasa, that "Tibetans will live happily in the great land of Tibet, and the Chinese will live happily in the great land of China."

As a Buddhist monk, my concern extends to all members of the human family and, indeed, to all sentient beings who suffer. I believe all suffering is caused by ignorance. People inflict pain on others in the selfish pursuit of their happiness or satisfaction. Yet true happiness comes from a sense of inner peace and contentment, which in turn must be achieved through the cultivation of altruism, of love and compassion and elimination of ignorance, selfishness and greed.

The problems we face today, violent conflicts, destruction of nature, poverty, hunger, and so on, are human-created problems which can be resolved through human effort, understanding and the development of a sense of brotherhood and sisterhood. We need to cultivate a universal responsibility for one another and the planet we share. Although I have found my own Buddhist religion helpful in generating love and compassion, even for those we consider our enemies, I am convinced that everyone can develop a good heart and a sense of universal responsibility with or without religion.

With the ever-growing impact of science on our lives, religion and spirituality have a greater role to play by reminding us of our humanity. There is no contradiction between the two. Each gives us valuable insights into the other. Both science and the teachings of the Buddha tell us of the fundamental unity of all things. This understanding is crucial if we are to take positive and decisive action on the pressing global concern with the environment. I believe all religions pursue the same goals, that of cultivating human goodness and bringing happiness to all human beings. Though the means might appear different the ends are the same. As we enter the final decade of this century I am optimistic that the ancient values that have sustained mankind are today reaffirming themselves to prepare us for a kinder, happier twenty-first century.

I pray for all of us, oppressor and friend, that together we succeed in building a better world through human understanding and love, and that in doing so we may reduce the pain and suffering of all sentient beings.

Thank you.

---

Available at http://nobelprize.org.

## DISCUSSION QUESTIONS
1. How does the Dalai Lama interpret the events of May–June in China?
2. What does he see as the relationship between Tibet and the Tiananmen Square democracy movement?
3. What does the Dalai Lama hope the Peace Prize may mean for the Tibetan cause?

**Eastern Europe**

# The Proclamation of Timişoara (March 1990)

*Leaders of Romania's 1989 revolution issued this proclamation shortly after the deaths of the Ceauşescus. The writers emphasized that the revolution did not end with the fall of the dictators and must be an ongoing process of transforma-*

*tion of the political and economic structures. In particular, the document insisted on a program of lustration, which would limit the future roles of former communist leaders and informers. Several of the former communist countries, including East Germany, Czechoslovakia, and Poland, instituted lustration legislation. Excerpts of the Proclamation are presented here.*

---

1. From its earliest hours the Revolution of Timişoara was directed not only against Ceauşescu, but, definitely, also against communism. "Down with communism!" was chanted several hundred times during all the days of the Revolution. In full agreement with the wish of the hundreds of millions of East European people we, too, called for the immediate abolishment of this totalitarian and failing social system. The ideal of our Revolution has been and is the return to the genuine values of European democracy and civilization.

2. All the social classes did participate in the Revolution of Timişoara. Workers, intellectuals, office workers, students, school-children, even villagers, who came to support the Revolution, were cut down by bullets side by side in the streets of Timişoara. We positively oppose the typically communist method of domination by spreading feuds among social classes and strata. . . .

3. People of all age-groups participated in the Revolution of Timişoara. Even if young people were preponderant, it is right to admit that people of all ages fought for the cause of the Revolution with the same daring. The list of victims, though incomplete, is a standing proof in this respect.

4. Side by side with the Romanians, there were Hungarians, Germans, Serbians, members of other ethnic groups who sacrificed their lives for the cause of the Revolution. They have all been coinhabiting our city in peace and goodwill for centuries. Timişoara is a European city where all the nationalities have rejected and reject nationalism. All the chauvinists of the country, no matter whether they are Romanians, Hungarians or Germans, are invited to come to Timişoara to a re-education course in the spirit of tolerance and mutual respect, the sole principles reigning in the future European House.

5. Already on the 16th of December, in the first hours of the Revolution, one of the most chanted slogans was "We want free elections!" The idea of political pluralism has been and is among the most cherished values of the people of Timisoara. It is our belief that without strong political parties genuine democracy, of a European kind, cannot exist. . . .

6. After four decades of exclusively communist education and propaganda, prejudices engendered by this ideology still haunt Romanians' consciences. The existence of such prejudices is not the bearer's guilt. Nevertheless, their manipulation by groups interested in resuscitating communism and bringing it back to power is a counter-revolutionary act. . . .

7. By no means did Timişoara start the Revolution against the entire communist regime and its whole nomenclature as an opportunity for a group of anti Ceauşescu dissidents within the RCP to rise to political power. Their presence in the leadership of the country renders the deaths of Timişoara's heroes useless. We may have accepted them ten years ago, if at the XII. party congress they would have joined Constantin Parvulescu and overthrown the dictatorial clan. But they had not done it, although they had had both the opportunity and the important positions that gave them prerogatives. On the contrary, some even obeyed the dictator's order to denigrate the dissident. Their cowardice cost us ten more years of dictatorship, the hardest of all the period, and a painful genocide.

8. As a consequence of the previous issue, we suggest that the electoral law should deny the former party workers and Security officers the right to be nominated as candidates on any list for the first three running legislatures. Their presence in the country's political life is the chief source of the tensions and suspicions that worry the Romanian society nowadays. Their absence from public life is absolutely necessary until the situation has been settled and national reconciliation has been effected. We also demand that in a special clause the electoral law should ban the former party activists from running for the position of President of the country. . . .

9. The people of Timişoara did not make the revolution to get higher wages or other material advantages. A strike would have

sufficient achieved these goals. We are all dissatisfied with the system of wages. . . . Once inflation is let loose, several years of efforts to curb it will be necessary. Only an increase in production, i.e. the quantity of goods in market, will make a general wage increase possible. Besides, the priority of the impoverished budget would be to rest a minimum standard of civilization. Immediate investments are necessary, for instance, in the public services of health and sanitation.

10. Although we strive to re-Europeanize Romania, we do not want to copy the western capitalist systems with their drawbacks and inequities. Still we positively uphold the idea of private initiative. The economic foundation of totalitarianism is the all-powerful state property. We shall never have political pluralism without economic pluralism. But one can hear voices that, in true communist spirit, define private initiative as "exploitation" and warn against the danger of the appearance of rich people. This is a way to stir up the envy of a lazy and dread of work of the former privileged people in the communist enterprises. . . .

11. Timişoara is determined to take economic and administrative decentralization seriously. A model of market-economy has already been put forward for testing, utilizing the powerful capacities and the competence of experts to be found in Timiş county. In order to attract foreign capital more quickly and more easily, chiefly as technology and special raw materials, and to create joint ventures, we urge that a branch of Foreign Trade Bank should be set up in Timişoara. A part of the hard currency incomes of the Romanian side in these joint ventures will be included in the workers' wages according to a percentage previously negotiated with the trade-union leaders. The payment in hard currency of a certain part of the wages will be a good material incentive for the workers. Moreover, passports will no longer be booklets worth keeping only in the drawer. Another positive consequence would be the fall of the free-market rate of hard currency, which will result in an immediate increase in the people's standard of living.

12. After the fall of the dictatorship all the Romanians living in exile were invited to return home to help reconstructing the

country. Some have already returned, others announced their intention. Unfortunately, there are still people who, instigated by obscure forces, abused the returned exiles, calling them "traitors" and provocatively asking them what they have eaten in the last ten years. This attitude does not do us credit at all. . . .

13. We do not agree with establishing December 22 as Romania's National Day. This is a way of immortalizing the dictator's person by celebrating a certain number of years since his fall. . . .

This Proclamation engendered by the necessity of making the Romanian nation acquainted with the ideals of the Revolution of Timişoara. It was a revolution made by the people, and only by it, with the interference of party activists and security agents. It was a genuine revolution, not a Coup d'Etat. It was definitely anticommunist, not only anti-Ceauşescu.

---

Available at http://www.ceausescu.org/ceausescu_texts/revolution/procl_tm_eng.htm.

## DISCUSSION QUESTIONS
1. What perceptions of the Romanian revolution do the document's authors want to correct?
2. The document's authors insist that the revolution is ongoing. What reforms do they believe are necessary for Romania's future?
3. To what extent are the authors attempting to curb Romanian nationalism?

# Mikhail Gorbachev, Speech Dissolving the Soviet Union (USSR) (December 25, 1991)

*With the loss of its satellite nations, the Soviet Union was plagued by sharp divisions among leaders. The country was dividing along nationalist lines, and there was widespread dissatisfaction that Gorbachev's programs had failed to bring economic relief to the citizenry. In August 1991, a failed coup attempt by hard-line Marxists weakened Gorbachev's power. The newly elected president of Russia, Boris Yeltsin, put down the coup and restored Gorbachev's office. However, by the end of the year, it had become clear that Yeltsin was the emerging leader, promising even more sweeping economic reforms. After Ukraine negotiated independence, Gorbachev announced the dissolution of the Soviet Union and his resignation from office.*

Dear compatriots, fellow citizens, as a result of the newly formed situation, creation of the Commonwealth of Independent States, I cease my activities in the post of the U.S.S.R. president. I am taking this decision out of considerations based on principle. I have firmly stood for independence, self-rule of nations, for the sovereignty of the republics, but at the same time for preservation of the union state, the unity of the country.

Events went a different way. The policy prevailed of dismembering this country and disuniting the state, with which I cannot agree. And after the Alma-Ata meeting and the decisions taken there, my position on this matter has not changed. Besides, I am convinced that decisions of such scale should have been taken on the basis of a popular expression of will.

Yet, I will continue to do everything in my power so that agreements signed there should lead to real accord in the society, (and) facilitate the escape from the crisis and the reform process. Addressing you for the last time in the capacity of president of the U.S.S.R., I consider it necessary to express my evaluation of the road we have traveled since 1985, especially as there are a lot of contradictory, superficial and subjective judgments on that matter.

Fate had it that when I found myself at the head of the state it was already clear that all was not well in the country. There is plenty of everything: land, oil and gas, other natural riches, and God gave us lots of intelligence and talent, yet we lived much worse than developed countries and keep falling behind them more and more.

The reason could already be seen: The society was suffocating in the vise of the command-bureaucratic system, doomed to serve ideology and bear the terrible burden of the arms race. It had reached the limit of its possibilities. All attempts at partial reform, and there had been many, had suffered defeat, one after another. The country was losing perspective. We could not go on living like that. Everything had to be changed radically.

The process of renovating the country and radical changes in the world turned out to be far more complicated than could be expected. However, what has been done ought to be given its due. This society acquired freedom, liberated itself politically and spiritually, and this is the foremost achievement which we have not yet understood completely, because we have not learned to use freedom.

However, work of historic significance has been accomplished. The totalitarian system which deprived the country of an opportunity to become successful and prosperous long ago has been eliminated. A breakthrough has been achieved on the way to democratic changes. Free elections, freedom of the press, religious freedoms, representative organs of power, a multiparty (system) became a reality; human rights are recognized as the supreme principle.

The movement to a diverse economy has started, equality of all forms of property is becoming established, people who work on the land are coming to life again in the framework of land reform, farmers have appeared, millions of acres of land are being given over to people who live in the countryside and in towns.

Economic freedom of the producer has been legalized, and entrepreneurship, shareholding, privatization are gaining momentum. In turning the economy toward a market, it is important to remember that all this is done for the sake of the individual. At this difficult time, all should be done for his social protection, especially for senior citizens and children.

We live in a new world. The Cold War has ended, the arms race has stopped, as has the insane militarization which mutilated our economy, public psyche and morals. The threat of a world war has been removed. Once again I want to stress that on my part everything was done during the transition period to preserve reliable control of the nuclear weapons.

We opened ourselves to the world, gave up interference into other people's affairs, the use of troops beyond the borders of the country, and trust, solidarity and respect came in response.

The nations and peoples of this country gained real freedom to choose the way of their self-determination. The search for a democratic reformation of the multinational state brought us to the threshold of concluding a new Union Treaty. All these changes demanded immense strain. They were carried out with sharp struggle, with growing resistance from the old, the obsolete forces.

The old system collapsed before the new one had time to begin working, and the crisis in the society became even more acute.

The August co[u]p brought the general crisis to its ultimate limit. The most damaging thing about this crisis is the breakup of the statehood. And today I am worried by our people's loss of the citizenship of a great country. The consequences may turn out to be very hard for everyone.

I am leaving the post with apprehension, but also with hope, with faith in you, your wisdom and force of spirit. We are the heirs of a great civilization, and its rebirth into a new, modern and dignified life now depends on one and all.

Some mistakes could surely have been avoided, many things could have been done better, but I am convinced that sooner or later our common efforts will bear fruit, our nations will live in a prosperous and democratic society.

I wish all the best to all of you.

---

Available at http://www.publicpurpose.com/lib-gorb911225.htm.

## DISCUSSION QUESTIONS

1. What does Gorbachev see as the main achievements of his leadership?
2. Why does Gorbachev believe that reform ultimately failed in the Soviet Union?

# Václav Havel, Five Years Later
# (November 1994)

*After leading the intellectual dissident community of Czechoslovakia and the 1989 "Velvet Revolution," Václav Havel was chosen by the still-communist legislature as the first non-communist president in four decades. He was subsequently elected by popular vote to this position in June 1990. In January 1993, the Czech and Slovak Republics parted in the "velvet divorce," and Havel was elected to the office of the President of the Czech Republic. In this speech, given five years after the 1989 revolutions and excerpted here, Havel reflected on his country's accomplishments as well as his disappointments, particularly the split with Slovakia.*

The speed and dynamics that marked the construction of the new democratic state led necessarily to improvisations that could only be tested along the way, to the search for unknown practices and also to the loss of old securities. The political scene was peopled by dissidents, who recruited from Charter 77 circles and who enjoyed the highest credit thanks to the open and risky dialogue they had held with the communist regime, but who had very little experience with the management of the structures of power. Most of them left politics after a time as they realized the roles they took upon themselves were temporary and many of them gradually returned to their original professions of artists, sociologists, scientists. Still, some of them became firmly rooted in politics and thus confirmed my conviction about the irreplaceable role of intellectuals among those who are changing this world. Nonetheless, there had quickly been established a pluralistic system of political parties, a functional parliament and government as well as the Constitutional Court. A number of international activities was conducted with a single goal: to extricate [the] Czech Republic from the Soviet block and to set up the closest possible links with the democratic West.

The key problem of the day—transformation of the totalitarian planned economy into the open market system—would not have been an easy one to solve if it were not for a group of economists who had used to meet in the dark days of totalit[arianism] and contemplate the task they were suddenly confronted with in 1989 due to the historical turn of events. They were not open opponents of the power, such as the group around Charter 77, but excellent experts who had a clear idea of how to restore in Czechoslovakia a modern type of market economy after forty years of communism. It is encouraging to see how quickly many people adapted to the new situation. Almost overnight there has emerged a stratum of businessmen in the Czech Republic and the method of voucher privatization of state assets created millions of shareholders, even though only few people actually knew what shares are about after those forty years.

The international results of the process of our integration into the European democratic structures are less satisfactory. I am afraid that the disintegration of the bipolar world caught both parties unprepared. The West had resisted the danger of communism for decades supporting all attempts for democratization and all the human rights movements in Central and Eastern Europe. It is no wonder that the West got used, after those forty years, to the static polarity East—West and was not at all ready for the possibility of the collapse of communism. I dare say that only very few were able to imagine the extent of the problems that were to explode the moment communism was to fall. Our first task was to break the old bonds: I remember chairing the suicidal Warsaw Pact Assembly meeting at the Prague Castle. The economic communist structures died away rather naturally. The price deregulation and abolishment of the Moscow-managed trade exchange deemed the tools devised to control the economies of Soviet satellites inefficient. The Council of Mutual Economic Assistance came tumbling down.

Reviewing the past five years from the perspective of our hopes and expectations, we must admit that we reckoned our integration into the family of European democracies would be faster. Following the dissolution of [the] Warsaw Pact, we hoped for the gradual establishment of European security structures, the core of which would be the North Atlantic Alliance. For Central Europe appeared in a queer situation: after the breakdown of bipolar Europe, the countries between the European Union and Russia feel caught in a vacuum. The collapse of the Soviet empire led to the disruption of the Soviet economic, political and security block. The attempts at full membership in NATO and in the European Union could not have been instantly successful. That causes some countries to strive for an accelerated process that would lead to their admission to the European integration structures. Such impatience may not always be fully understood but it is only an expression of a bitter historical experience. And against the background of the traumas we have suffered under fascism and communism, a certain amount of impatience should be understandable.

\* \* \*

Still, I do have to stress that it will not suffice to keep knocking on the Western doors and emphasizing that we share the same values, that we too are Europe and that we expect greater broadmindedness, higher speed and more courage (though we could do with more courage, higher speed and great broad-mindedness) from the European Union. It is important that we do not only profess these values verbally, but that we also—after those four decades of communism when those values were suppressed—really revive them, accept them for our own, that we work on ourselves and on our societies. I believe our participation in UNPROFOR corps as well [as] our role of a temporary member of the UN Security Council bear evidence to this endeavour of ours.

And there is yet another principle I cannot fail to mention, a value that in a way penetrates all the others. It is the sense of shared responsibility for the affairs of this world that prevents us from concentrating only on ourselves, on who will help us and defend us, on who will protect us and that makes us offer our participation, accept our share of responsibility for European as well as global affairs. These are the moral foundations that should facilitate the particulars I have been contemplating here: democracy, the rule of law, market economy, civil society.

Looking back over those five years, naturally, I cannot overlook what our society has failed to accomplish. One such failure, in my opinion, is the division of our state. Only very few would have realized in the moments of revolutionary enthusiasm that the latent yearning of the Slovak nation for an independent state was so deep that it would soon jeopardize the cohesion of Czechoslovakia. The end of the common state was felt by many people to be a trauma but looking back I must appreciate the calm and peaceful process of the division. We do know how unusual it is for a state to divide so peacefully on the basis of agreements, as in our case. Division or disintegration of states is usually connected with civil unrest if not war. In our case it was the result of free elections and different election programs of our respective political forces. Complicated negotiations conducted by the Czech and Slovak political representatives resulted in the agreement to divide the state. Both republics are connected with numerous ties—families, economic links, customs union, traditional cultural links. What is most important is the lack of animosity between the two nations. I would not like to create the impression that I am glad for the division and I have in fact done my best to prevent it, but if there was no other way, I cannot but feel satisfied that the common state was dissolved in such a civilized manner.

On the other hand, there are disturbing phenomena: five years ago we could not have anticipated the tragedy that would be caused by militant nationalism, xenophobia, racism, criminal fight for ethnic [cleansing] manifested in such a perverted form in Bosnia-Herzegovina. The explosion of these darkest of human features took us by surprise. Here too, we can see the relationship between communist collectivism and nationalistic collectivism in which anonymous masses will provide refuge to frustrated helpless individuals, who have only exchanged their banners and slogans. This, too, is related to the disintegration of the false values and certainties of the communist regime. The new situation encourages the search for substitute culprits, all kinds of radicalism, the necessity to hide in the anonymous collective whether group-like or ethnic, the hatred of the world, the need of self-assurance at any cost, unprecedented egoism springing from the feeling that now everything is allowed, the search for a collective and easily defined enemy, political extremism and the most primitive cult of consumption. Yet, despite this intimidating list of demons that permanently threaten democracy, I do not see a reason for pessimism. The existence of such phenomena only presents us with yet another challenge.

Originally written in November 1994 for World Media. Currently available at the official website of Václav Havel, http://www.vaclavhavel.cz/index .php?sec=3&id=4.

## DISCUSSION QUESTIONS

1. According to Havel, what have been the Czech Republic's most important achievements since the fall of communism?
2. Where does Havel believe that the Czech Republic and the region have failed?

# Jiřina Siklová, Why Western Feminism Isn't Working in the Czech Republic (1999)

*Jiřina Siklová is a sociologist and founder of gender studies in the Czech Republic. An early signer of Charter 77, she worked closely with the dissident community before 1989. Since the revolution, she has brought public attention to women's issues. In this essay, excerpted below, she discusses her analysis of why Western feminism has remained unpopular in the Czech Republic. In doing so, she also highlights Western misunderstandings about the revolutions of 1989 and the particular needs of women in the post-socialist countries.*

So why is Western feminism so unwelcome in the Czech Republic? In comparison with Western women, Czech women are very emancipated, but they don't want to recognize it. They firmly reject feminist ideology, almost as if they were afraid that if they gave a name to their status, the situation would change. Women in the Czech Republic generally occupy an important position in the family and they have far more responsibility for the family and its finances than men or most feminists in the West. At the same time, however, they accept a seemingly second-class status with a strange form of affected humility. Under socialism, most women more or less managed the dual role of worker-mother. They grumbled about it, but they were also proud of it. When Western feminists try to tell Czech women that the family is not the most important issue facing their gender today, what they are doing is taking the aura of martyrdom away from Czech women. Perhaps that is why feminism is most firmly rejected by middle-aged Czech women, who grew up under socialism and are now involved in business. Such women have attained a higher social status and are now influencing the image of Czech women as a whole.

In contrast, younger Czech women, especially university students, are interested in feminism and want to study it. Perhaps they understand that this country, which used to be very paternalistic, will one day turn into a society in which ownership relations will become paramount. In such a society, men would be even more powerful as property owners or entrepreneurs, and gender discrimination could become a problem. Similar developments in the West led to the birth of the feminist movement.

Most of the qualified criticism of feminism that exists in the Czech Republic is based on our recent experiences with socialism as well as on our experiences with the fight to preserve the Czech nation. Over the past two centuries, Czech men and women had more common interests than their Western counterparts. Over the years, these common interests (or enemies) changed according to surrounding circumstances: in the 19th and early 20th centuries, it was the fight for the survival of the Czech language in the face of the Austro-Hungarian Empire; during World War II, it was the resistance to the Nazi German occupation; and finally, during the Cold War, it was the resistance to the communist regime. In the latter phase, since everything had been nationalized, women did not feel aversion toward men as owners or employers but rather toward the regime as the sole employer in the country and toward the overbearing Communist Party. Neither of these feelings of aversion were based on gender distinctions.

## Sisters and Comrades

Czech women who are familiar with Western feminism criticize it for its ideological nature as well as for the manner in which it posits a universal solution for the problems of women all over the world. Slogans like "Sisterhood is international" remind us of the slogans we used to hear about the working class. Years of communism and now postcommunism have convinced us that there is no universal worker whose interests are the same in Beijing, Moscow, Manchester, and Prague. We have also come to understand that dividing people up according to social status (which could also be inherited) did not solve our problems, nor did it bring us happiness. How then could some sort of international sisterhood resolve our problems?

In short, many Western feminists appear too leftist to us and seem to be oriented toward an ideology that we just got rid of. Their criticism of Western democracy makes us uneasy because that is precisely the kind of system we would like to have in our own country. In fact, Czech women tend to be more right wing than their male compatriots. According to surveys conducted by Czech sociologist Marie Cermeková, women in this country tend to vote for right-wing parties more often than men. Furthermore, they have tended to hold on to their jobs. The number of employed women in the Czech Republic has decreased by only 3 percent since 1989.

Some misunderstandings arise from the fact that many Western feminists believe that Soviet-style socialism had resolved the problem of women's equality in Eastern Europe and that its collapse was a setback for women in this region. They criticize us for not fighting for the "gains" of socialism which the former regime bestowed on us. They argue that socialism enabled women to obtain the same level of education and employment as men, thereby proving that women are just as capable as men. They don't understand that in our country, both men and women value the freedom of expression and the free market they have today more than they valued the "security" that the socialist regime offered them. Even though we may not be extremely well-versed in theoretical Marxism, we still don't have any illusions about the "dictatorship of the proletariat" because we know what that means in practice better than any Western feminist. While it is true that Lenin considered the emancipation of women to be an integral part of socialist progress, he also emphasized that the interests of women should be subordinate to the interests of the working class. If women wanted equality, they had to join the ready-made world which consisted of social structures and power relations created by men and mainly for men. The Leninist program told women: "Adjust yourselves to our plan, work, and achieve what we have achieved and then we'll consider you to be equals." No national or racial minority would agree with such demands in this day and age. Anybody who tried to implement such ideas today would be accused of violating basic human rights.

Thus, the ideology of socialism replaced the "patriarchy" of capitalist ownership with the authority of the totalitarian state. Private rule was replaced with so-called public patriarchy. In order to secure control over all its citizens, the socialist state decreased the dependency of individual women on their husbands by introducing state support programs for mothers. For that reason, women in socialist countries were more interested in politics than women in the West at that time. Thanks to quotas established by the Communist Party, women had greater representation in parliament under that regime than they do today (women made up 29 percent of the communist parliament compared with 15 percent today). However, this does not mean that women in the Czech Republic were more involved in politics under the previous regime than they are today. The parliament of the communist era was not engaged in real politics as we understand the term in democratic countries. Perhaps this is why Czech women today are against the establishment of gender quotas for public legislatures.

From Center for Digital Discourse and Culture at Virginia Tech. Available at http://www.cddc.vt.edu/feminism/cz4.html.

## DISCUSSION QUESTIONS
1. In what ways does Siklová see Czech women as emancipated?
2. Why did many Czechs reject Western feminism in the decade after the fall of Communism?

# Zoltan Barany, Orphans of Transition: Gypsies in Eastern Europe (1998)

*The Roma (gypsy) minority of Eastern Europe has been called by political scientist Zoltan Barany the "orphans of transition." Nationalist sentiment that emerged after the fall of communism often targeted Roma, often violently. Since the fall of communism, Roma rights organizations have emerged and many national and international leaders have called on their citizens to respect the human rights of this community. However, the Roma have higher rates of unemployment and poverty than the national majorities, and there is widespread prejudice against the group. In the article excerpted here, Barany analyzes why Roma in Eastern Europe have not benefited from the transition from communism.*

---

For the approximately six million Roma (Gypsies) who live in Eastern Europe, the transition from communism has been an altogether deplorable experience. Though entire sections of society (unskilled laborers, pensioners, and so on) have been hurt by the marketization processes that began nearly a decade ago, none has been more adversely affected than the Roma.

A wide variety of long-marginalized groups whose exclusion had been based on ethnicity, gender, sexual orientation, or other grounds had greeted the fall of the *ancien régime* enthusiastically, expecting an end to state-sanctioned discrimination and societal prejudices. On the whole, marginal groups—and especially ethnic minorities—have been more successful in acquiring rights and stopping discriminatory practices in countries where democratization has advanced rapidly than in countries where the process has been sluggish. One feature common to all East European states, however, is the desperate situation of the Gypsies.

Reliable estimates put the world's Gypsy population at about 10 million. Europe is home to about 8 million Roma, almost three-fourths of whom reside in Eastern Europe. Another million live in the United States. In a number of Western democracies, the Roma continues to suffer discrimination—some of it de jure, but most of it de facto. Even though the Roma of Western Europe tend to be at the bottom of the socioeconomic scale in the countries where they live, their standards of living are far superior to those of their Eastern European brethren.

In Eastern Europe, a relatively prosperous region by global standards, the vast majority of Gypsies live in misery and want. Prejudice against them is wide and deep, and, on several occasions since 1989, has led to vigilante-style violence and pogroms. The Roma's progress in attaining political representation in proportion

to the size of their communities has been halting at best; their political power remains minimal. Perhaps most troubling of all, the
key markers of their predicament are nearly identical in all of
Eastern Europe. Their situation poses a threat to the democratic
society that political and civic elites aspire to consolidate.

[ * * * ]

## The Travails of Postcommunism

Eastern Europe's gradual metamorphosis from an inefficient, cen-
trally planned economic system to a market- and performance-
oriented one has essentially reversed whatever socioeconomic
headway the Gypsies made under state socialism, and has led to
profound and widespread poverty among them. This phenomenon
is an unfortunate but logical consequence of the postcommunist
economic transition.

In every East European state the full-employment principle of
state socialism has been gradually replaced by that of labor ratio-
nalization. In practice, this means that individuals whose labor is
expendable for a given enterprise or production unit are laid off.
People with no marketable skills and weak employment records are
hit especially hard. Romani communities have suffered far more
from this change than others because the large majority of Gypsies
are unskilled laborers whose work performance has often been
hampered by irregular attendance and low morale. In the postcommunist period, the Roma tend to be fired first and hired last, both
because of these objective circumstances and because of remaining
prejudice against them. One of the underlying problems is that
most Roma lack the kind of training that would make them attrac-
tive to prospective employers. As János Wolfart, the former head of
the National Ethnic Minorities Office in Budapest, asked, "How do
you *re*train someone with no convertible skills?"

In parts of contemporary Eastern Europe, unemployment
among Gypsies is staggering. In some particularly underdeveloped
regions of Slovakia, Hungary, Romania, and the former Yugoslavia
it approaches 90 to 100 percent. With unemployment benefits, social security, and welfare payments erratically available at best,

many Roma have turned to begging, prostitution, and crime. Roma criminal activities are reported extensively and often unfairly in the media, thereby adding to the Gypsies' alienation.

This situation is expected to get worse, as Romani school attendance has plummeted across the region. Communist social workers often herded reluctant Gypsy children to school, something that most contemporary East European states no longer have the resources to do. The shrinking Romani presence in higher education is also troubling, for it stifles the growth of the nascent Gypsy middle class and robs the Romani community of role models. There have been attempts in Hungary, Slovakia, and elsewhere to finance secondary and postsecondary education specifically for Gypsy children and their teachers from public and private funds. Such efforts have been few in number, however, and are unlikely to provide a satisfactory solution to the issue, particularly given the rapid growth of the Romani population.

The emergence of extreme nationalism since 1989 has at times made the Gypsies (as well as other ethnic and racial minorities) targets of violence. Across the region, "skinheads" and ordinary citizens motivated by Gypsy crimes, by the alleged wealth of a small number of Romani entrepreneurs, and in some cases by pure racism, have killed dozens of Roma and burned down hundreds of their dwellings, in many cases under the eyes of indifferent police authorities. Although in recent years more vigorous police involvement has made such attacks less frequent, the loss of physical security combined with their increasing poverty has driven tens of thousands of Roma to seek asylum in Western Europe and North America, thereby transforming the "Gypsy problem" from a national into an international issue. In 1997 alone, thousands of Roma from Bulgaria, the Czech Republic, Romania, and Slovakia requested political asylum in Canada, Germany, Ireland, and the United Kingdom, straining relations (resulting in renewed visa requirements) between their countries of origin and of destination.

Another profound and, for once, positive change in Romani marginality in the postcommunist period has been the diminution of their political exclusion. Like other previously disenfranchised groups, the Gypsies have sought to capitalize on the opportunity to organize and gain interest representation through participation in the political process. For a number of reasons, however, they have been remarkably unsuccessful in furthering the Romani cause.

Successful ethnic political mobilization is contingent upon several criteria that the Roma do not satisfy at present, nor can be expected to satisfy in the foreseeable future. First, Gypsy ethnic identity is extremely weak. According to a recent monograph on the subject, "with the exception of Gypsy intellectuals who run the Rom[ani] political parties, the Rom[a] do not have an ethnic identity" at all. Even settling on a precise ethnic definition is difficult, since the Roma vary considerably in language, dialect, lifestyle, occupation, socioeconomic status, and religion. Most Gypsies do not consider themselves part of a cohesive ethnic group, but identify instead with the subgroup to which they belong. In northeastern Bulgaria alone, there are nineteen Romani tribes, each with its particular customs, traditional trades, and other distinctive features. A large proportion of East European Gypsies (at least 80 percent in Hungary, for instance) speak no Romani at all. Furthermore, until a few years ago, Romani was not even a written language, which helps to explain most Gypsies' ignorance about and lack of interest in their background. Second, the Roma have neither a history of mobilization nor a set of political resources to draw upon. Third, when it comes to the highly important "conventional" factors that determine a group's political success (leadership, programs and objectives, party organizations and participation), the Roma have thus far been singularly ineffectual.

*Journal of Democracy*, 9, no. 3 (1998): 142–56.

## DISCUSSION QUESTIONS

1. What does Barany mean when he calls the Roma "orphans of transition"?
2. Have there been some benefits for Roma minorities since the fall of communism?

# Part V
## For Further Reading

### China

Brook, Timothy. *Quelling the People: The Military Suppression of the Beijing Democracy Movement.* Stanford, CA: Stanford University Press, 1998. Focuses on the military aspects of the suppression, including detailed accounts of the troops' entry into Beijing.

Calhoun, Craig. *Neither Gods nor Emperors: Students and the Struggle for Democracy in China.* Berkeley: University of California Press, 1994. A sophisticated analysis by a leading sociologist, though not a China specialist. Situates the movement into existing literature on social protest.

Han' Minzhu and Sheng Hua, eds. *Cries for Democracy: Writings and Speeches from the 1989 Chinese Democracy Movement.* Princeton, NJ: Princeton University Press, 1990. The most complete collection of primary sources from the Beijing Student Movement. The editor's pseudonym translates to "Chinese Democracy."

Liu Binyan, with Ruan Ming and Xu Gang. *"Tell the World": What Happened in China and Why,* trans. Henry L. Epstein. New York: Pantheon, 1989. One of the first eyewitness accounts to be published. Liu Binyan is an important journalist in the PRC [People's Republic of China].

Shen Tong. *Almost a Revolution: The Story of a Chinese Student's Journey from Boyhood to Leadership in Tiananmen Square.* Ann Arbor: University of Michigan, 1998. Autobiography of one of the movement's student leaders, emphasizing the personal aspect of modern Chinese history and politics.

*The Tiananmen Papers: The Chinese Leadership's Decision to Use Force against Their Own People—In Their Own Words,* comp. Zhang Liang, eds. Andrew J. Nathan and Perry Link. New York: Public Affairs,

2001. Controversial compilation of original documents smuggled out of China that show the inner workings of the decisions made at the upper levels of the PRC [People's Republic of China] government.

Wasserstrom, Jeffrey N. and Elizabeth Perry. *Popular Protest and Political Culture in Modern China,* 2nd ed. Boulder, CO: Westview Press, 1994. An important compilation that includes Jeffrey Wasserstrom and Joseph Esherick's article on 1989 as "political theater."

Zhao, Dingxin. *The Power of Tiananmen: State-Society Relations and the 1989 Beijing Student Movement.* Chicago: University of Chicago Press, 2001. A sophisticated social science analysis of the movement.

## Eastern Europe

Garton Ash, Timothy. *The Magic Lantern: The Revolution of '89 Witnessed in Warsaw, Budapest, Berlin, and Prague.* New York: Vintage Books, 1993.

Havel, Václav. *To the Castle and Back.* New York: Vintage Books, 2008.

Kenney, Padraic. *A Carnival of Revolution: Central Europe 1989.* Princeton, NJ: Princeton University Press, 2003.

Rosenberg, Tina. *The Haunted Land: Facing Europe's Ghosts after Communism.* New York: Vintage Books, 1996.

Siani-Davies, Peter. *The Romanian Revolution of December 1989.* Ithaca, NY: Cornell University Press, 2005.

Stokes, Gale. *The Walls Came Tumbling Down: The Collapse of Communism in Eastern Europe.* New York: Oxford University Press, 1993.

Wałęsa, Lech. *The Struggle and the Triumph: An Autobiography.* New York: Arcade Publishing, 1992.

## World

Clark, Nancy L. and William H. Worger. *South Africa: The Rise and Fall of Apartheid.* Harlow, England: Pearson Longman, 2004.

Hagopian, Frances and Scott P. Mainwaring, eds. *The Third Wave of Democratization in Latin America: Advances and Setbacks.* Cambridge, UK: Cambridge University Press, 2005.

Mandela, Nelson. *Long Walk to Freedom: The Autobiography of Nelson Mandela.* Boston: Little, Brown, 1994.

# CREDITS

# INDEX